CW01668484

Knitting with Giant Needles

Simple projects to knit and crochet

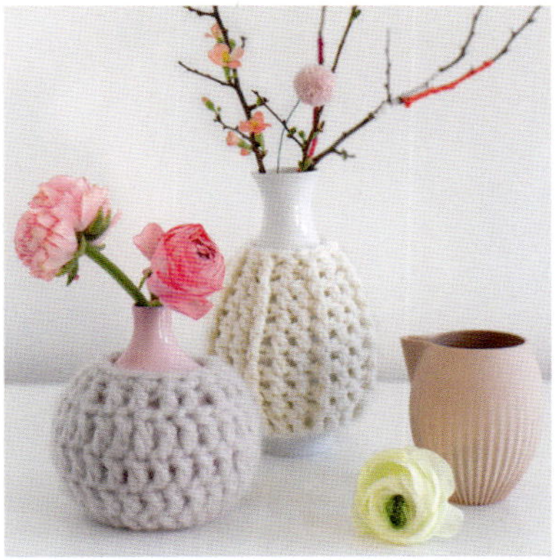

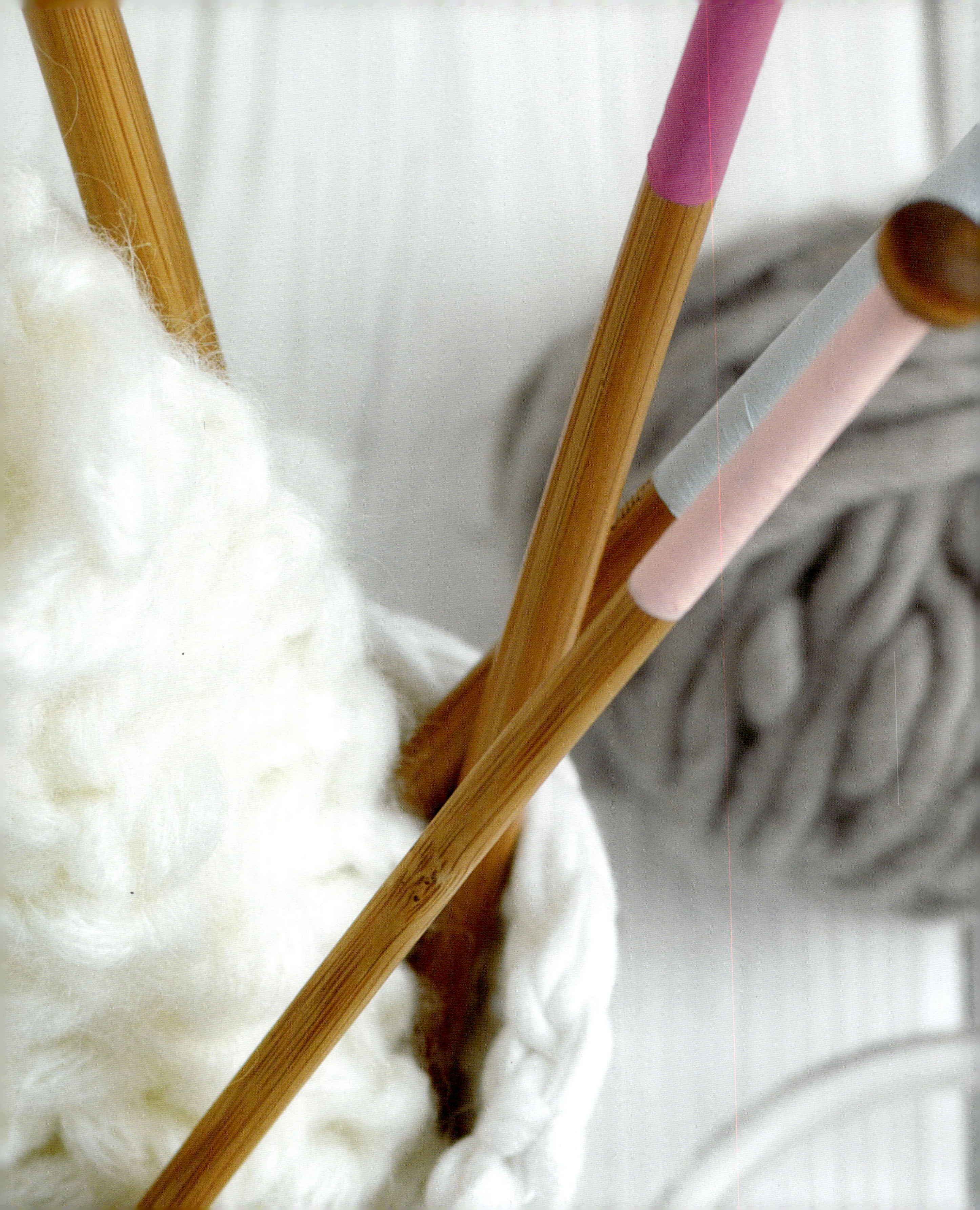

Hanna Charlotte Erhorn

Knitting with Giant Needles

Simple projects to knit and crochet

DK
DORLING KINDERSLEY

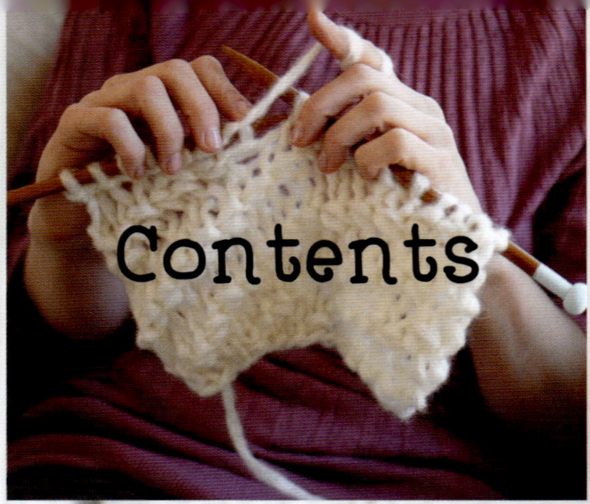

Contents

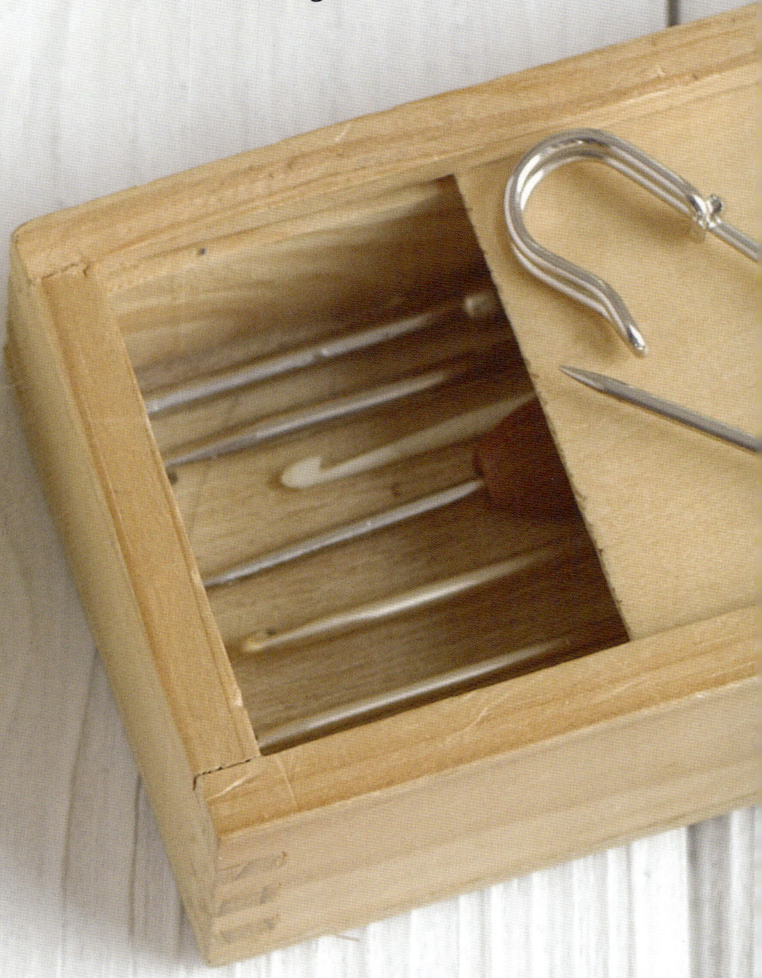

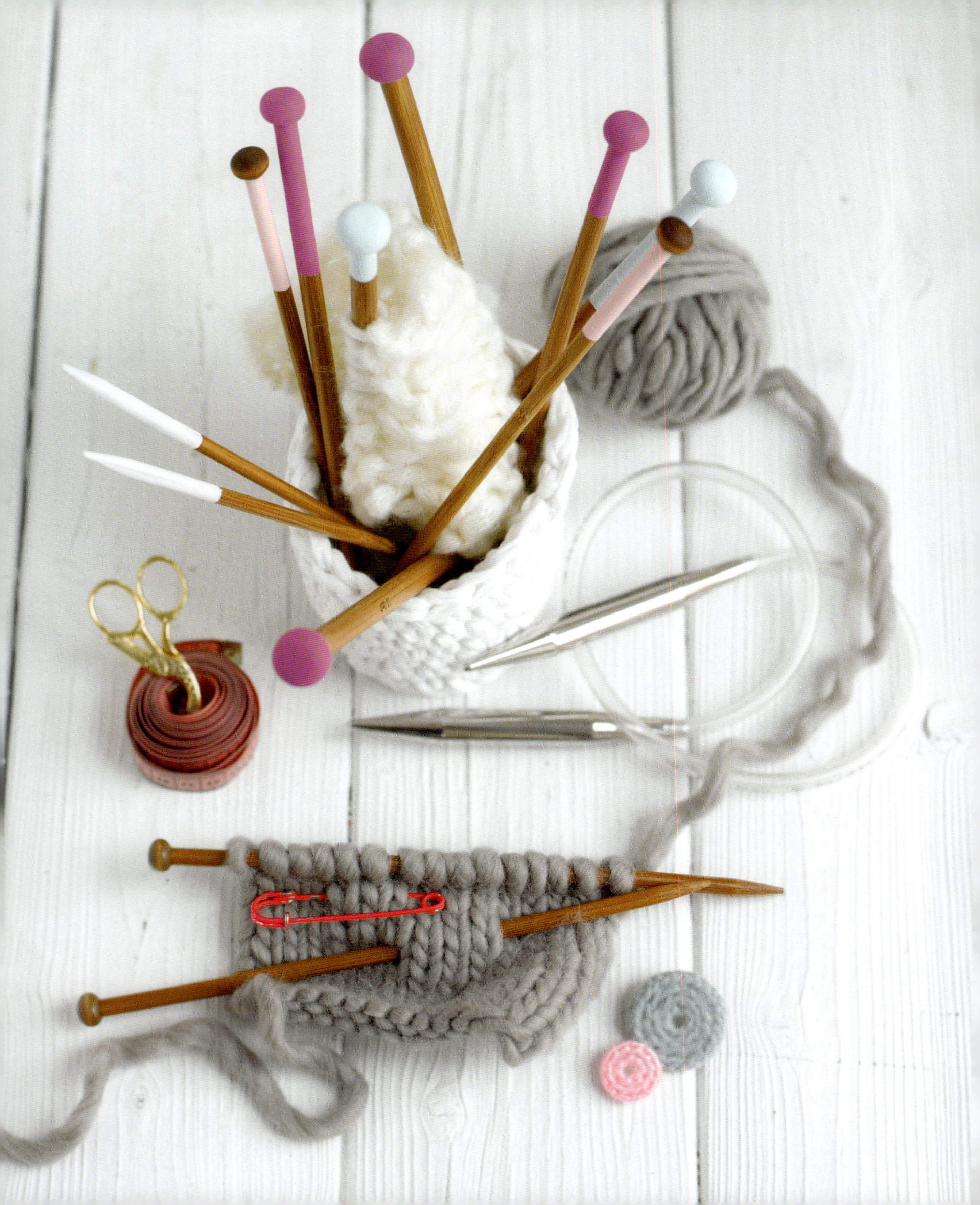

Chunky needles and yarns

I love knitting and crocheting. For me there is nothing nicer than sitting up half the night, all comfy and cosy on the couch, armed with needles and fabulous wool, working out new patterns. The great thing about it is that your mind and hands are kept busy, and you end up proudly producing something that is really special. It is both relaxing and stimulating at the same time. Throw in a chat with friends and a pot of tea or coffee, and new items of clothing or unique home accessories begin to take shape in next to no time.

With big needles and chunky yarns you can rustle up something wonderful, without it being time-consuming. For this book I have developed a range of projects to bring a cosy glow to you and your home: all it takes is a bit of flair and beautiful wool. Many of them are suitable for beginners as well. These easy to moderately difficult projects are simple to make with the help of the detailed descriptions and the step-by-step instructions in the quick guide to knitting and crocheting at the end of the book (see pp.84–95). All the projects give an approximate indication of the length of time each one will take to complete – after all, we get most satisfaction from any handicraft work when it produces rapid results.

Thick needles

The vast range of different needles and hooks for knitting and crocheting can be bewildering for beginners: as well as sets of double-pointed needles, there are single-pointed and circular needles, all of which can be made of metal, plastic, wood, or bamboo. It is generally left up to users to decide which type they prefer. The instructions give details of the ones I have used for the projects in this book.

The needle or hook size will depend on the yarn, your chosen project, and your own knitting style. The higher the number on the needle (diameter of the needle measured in mm), the larger the knitted stitch will be. Real knitting fans have even been known to make jumbo knitting needles out of broom handles. Our projects use needle and hook sizes ranging from 5mm (UK6/US8) to 20mm (US35), though I have also used smaller ones for the knitted and crocheted necklaces and bracelets. The techniques applied make them look bulky anyway.

Thick yarns

Thick yarns refer to those used with needle sizes 5.5mm (UK5/US9) and over. Sizes 8mm (UK0/US11) and above are used to knit extra-thick yarn. As a rule of thumb, the thicker the yarn, the thicker the knitting needle or crochet hook. You can often find the recommended needle size for a yarn printed on its ballband. However, this is only meant to act as a guide, because the needle size is not the only factor involved. Different materials and yarns of different ply behave differently when they are actually knitted.

The knitting will be looser and more open and stretchy if you use a needle that is larger in relation to the yarn. If you use thicker yarns with thinner needles, you will get very tight knitting and crochet work. So, depending on how it will be used, my instructions often give different needle sizes from the ones specified on the ballband.

Not all yarns come in the desired thickness, but, of course, you can combine several thinner yarns together to make one thick strand. To knit a double strand from one ball of yarn, pull out the other end from the middle of the ball, so that you are knitting with the beginning and the end of the yarn at the same time. If you like, you can even make your own super chunky yarn using a French knitter or (if you are really pushed for time) a knitting mill. These make striking accessories, such as the necklaces on page 68.

Synthetic or natural fibres?

The quality of the yarn is also important. Synthetic fibres are good for sturdy, fuzz-free, robust home accessories. Soft, cuddly items such as scarves and clothing are best made with yarn from animal hair, such as mohair, merino, or alpaca. These yarns are flexible and bulky and also retain the heat. Cotton and other natural fibres may be firm and resilient, but they are very heavy if used for thick knitting.

A combination of synthetic and natural fibres in one yarn allows you to enjoy the benefits of both. This type of yarn is often soft on the skin as well as being easy-care. And when buying yarn, make sure that all the balls of a particular colour have the same batch number, as the shade can vary slightly from one batch to the next.

Useful accessories

You will need a blunt-ended needle for sewing in strands of yarn and joining sections together. It is also worth having a small supply of pretty buttons and ribbons for decorating and fastening the knitted and crocheted sections. If you have needles but don't know their thickness, you can measure them using a needle gauge. A row counter is useful for keeping track of rows, and stitch markers indicate the start of a round of crochet (or you can use a safety pin).

Finishing touches

To finish off, you can stretch or steam the work to give the stitching a more even look. This works best with yarns made from natural fibres. Spray the knitting with water, stretch it out to shape on an ironing board (keeping it in place with pins), and leave it to dry completely. Alternatively you can gently steam it with an iron, but make sure the iron does not come into contact with the item. Then, leave it to cool down and dry. Always save a ballband from the yarn of a finished work, as it contains important care instructions.

Substituting yarn

If you want to use a different yarn from the one specified in the instructions, choose one that is very similar in weight and length, and knit a tension sample. The number of stitches and rows should match those given for the original yarn as closely as possible.

To work out how much of the new yarn you will need, do not go by the weight, as it varies according to the yarn. For instance, 1m (39in) of cotton yarn can weigh more than twice as much as the same length of a mohair yarn.

To calculate how much yarn you need for the project you have in mind, multiply the length of a ball (find it on the ballband) by the number of balls required. Buy the same total length of the yarn you want to use (adding a bit extra, to be on the safe side). Be sure to keep the receipts for your yarn purchases, as you can usually return unused balls of yarn within a pretty generous period of time if the ballbands are intact.

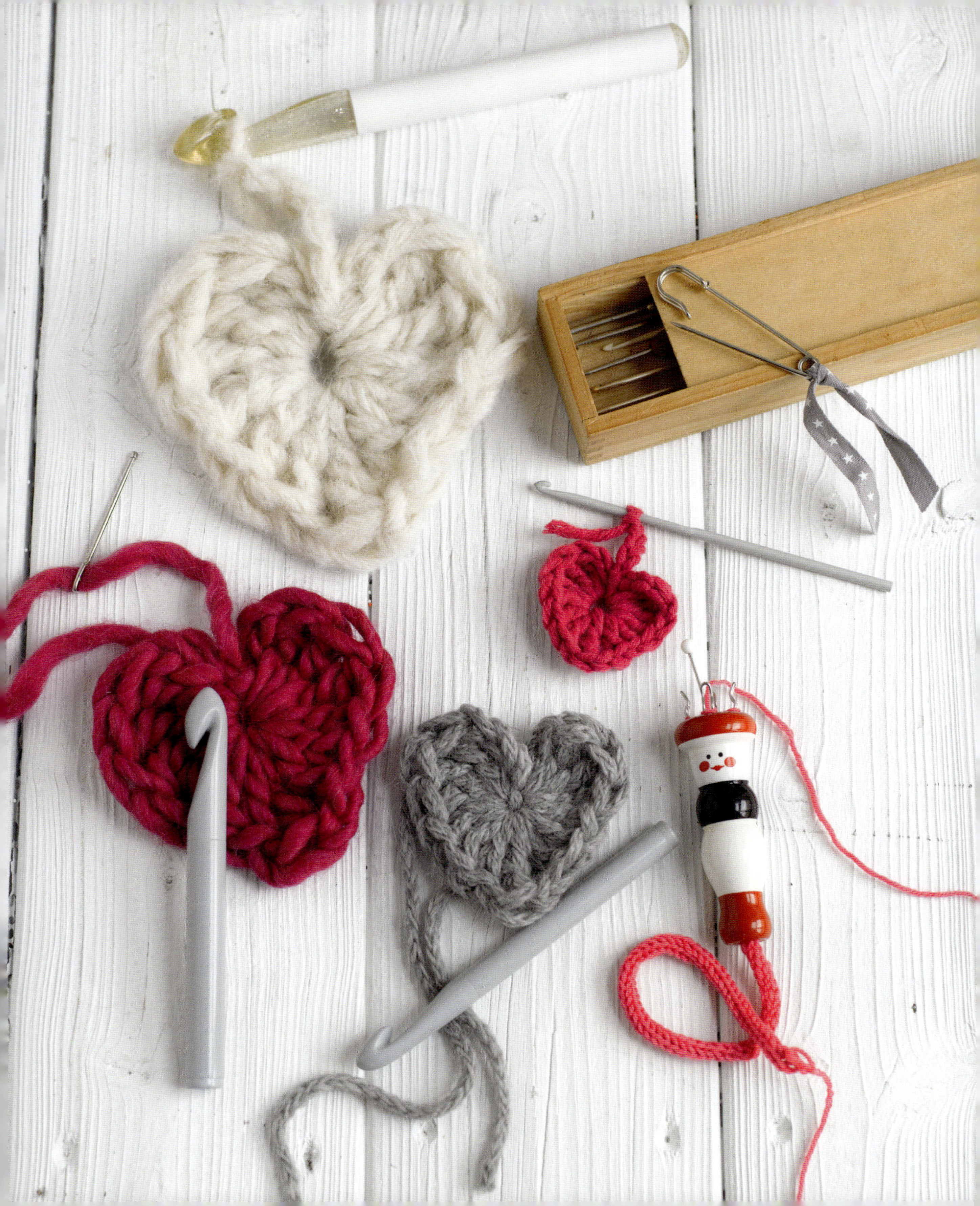

For the home

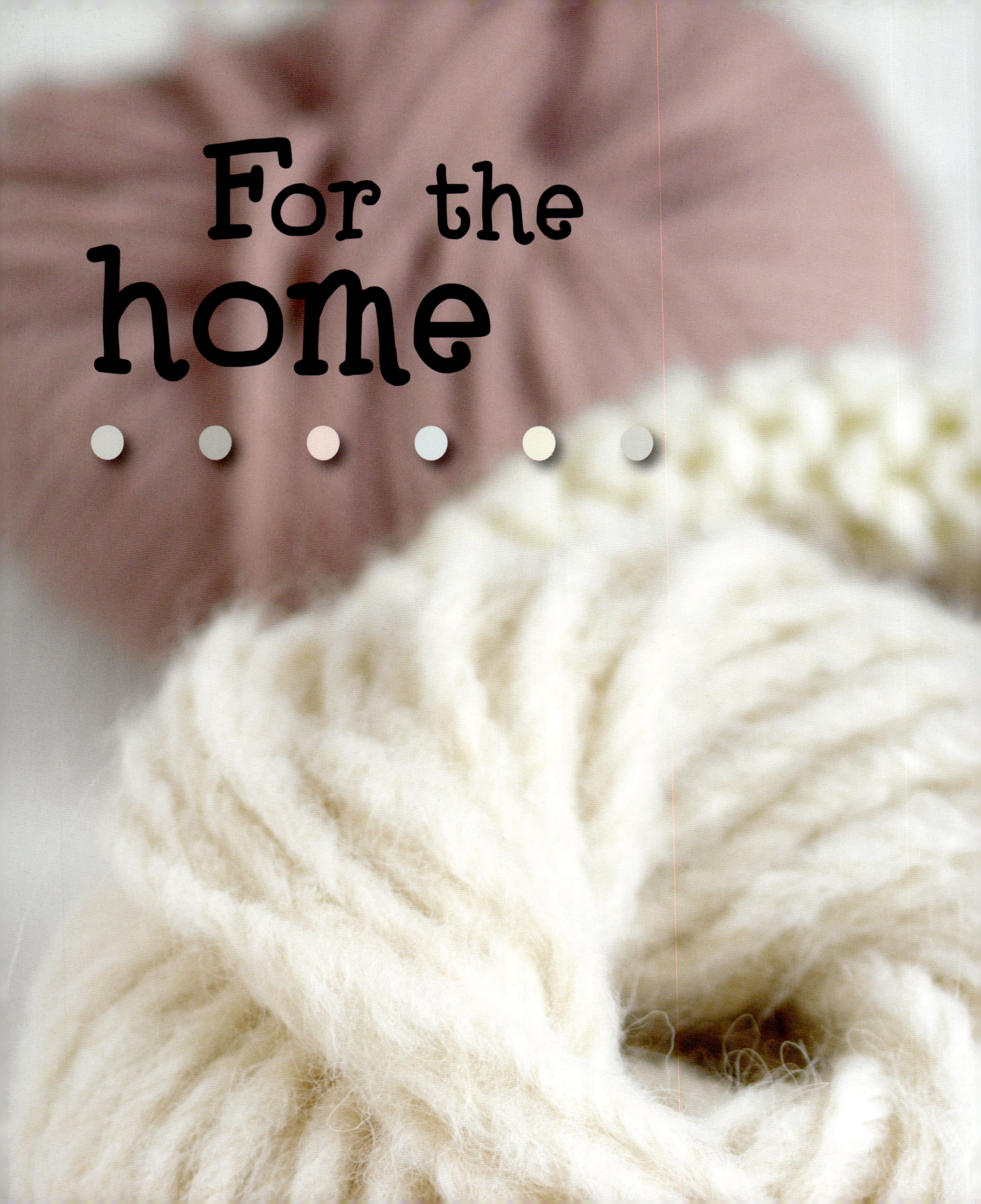

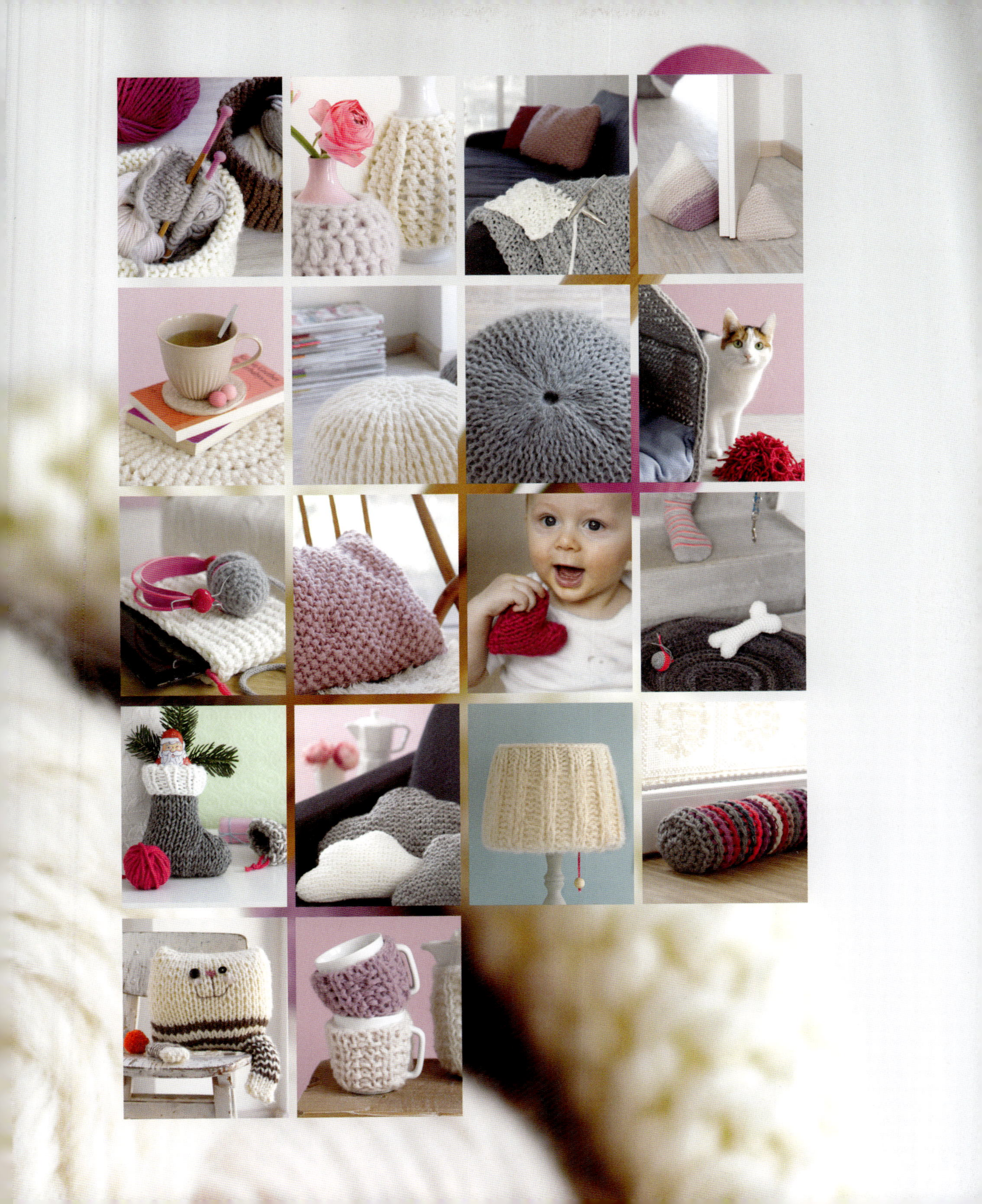

Soft baskets

TIME 1½–2 hours

Moderate

SIZE Diameter 25cm (9¾in), height 17cm (6¾in)

Materials

Yarn

Schachenmayr original Bravo Big, 200g each in 00110 (taupe) and 00102 (natural)

Other items

1 pair of 9mm (UK00/US13) needles

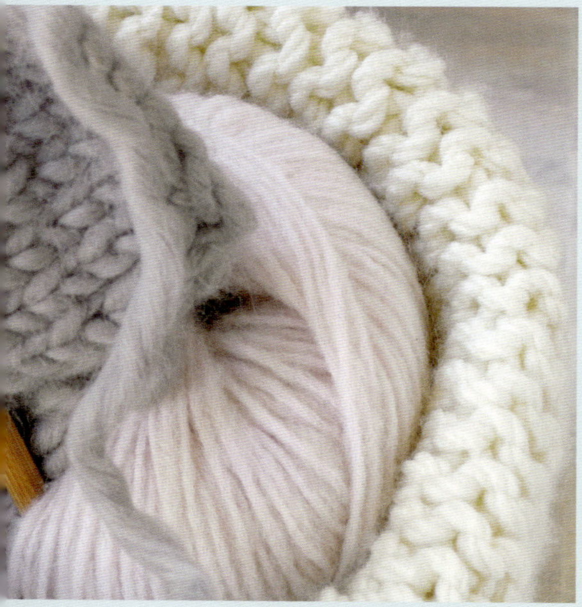

For a thick, rounded top edge on the white basket, fold over the edge either to the outside or to the inside, as in the photo above. The white basket will then be the same height as the brown one.

Instructions

Both baskets are knitted in garter stitch. The rounded bottom of the basket is achieved by knitting shortened rows. The number of stitches needed for the slightly smaller brown basket is given in brackets.
Cast on 32 (22) stitches.

Row 1: K29 (20), leave rem sts on needle, turn, and knit back along the row.
Row 2: K26 (18), leave rem sts on needle, turn, and knit back along the row.
Row 3: K23 (16), leave rem sts on needle, turn, and knit back along the row.
Row 4: K all sts, turn, and knit back. Rep rows 1–4 11 times.

Sew an invisible side seam using mattress stitch (see p.89). Draw the stitches at the bottom together with a strand of yarn.

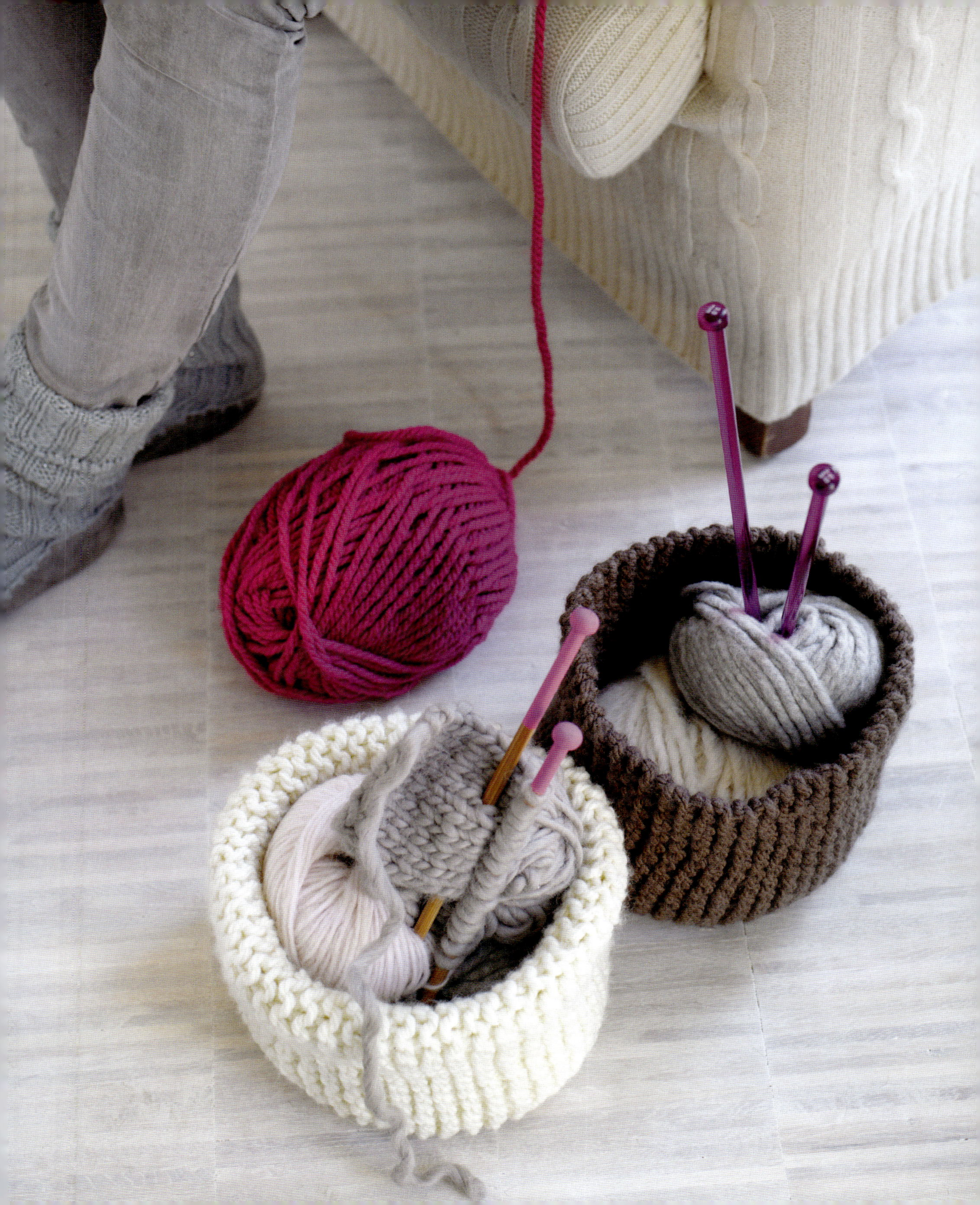

Vase covers

TIME 30 minutes

Easy

SIZE To fit any size; heights 12cm (5in) and 18cm (7in) shown here

Materials

Yarn

Schachenmayr select Silk Wool, 50g each in 07125 (natural) and 07119 (powder)
Work with two strands of yarn.

Other items

8mm hook

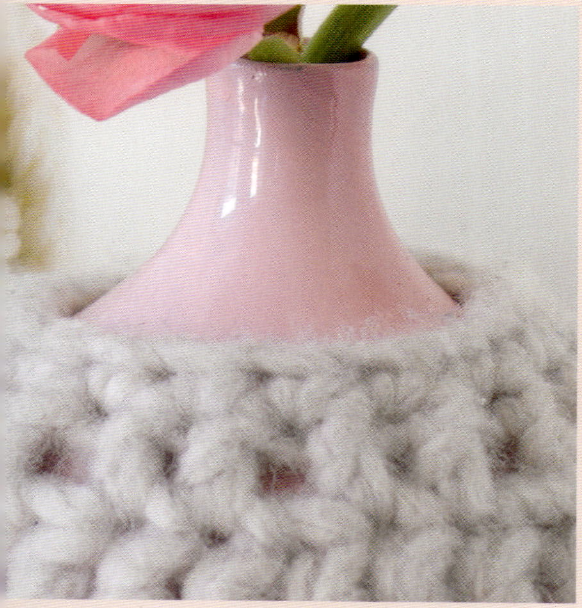

In this pattern, decreasing is done by working a treble crochet in the next-but-one stitch of the previous round rather than in the next stitch. To make an increase, work two trebles in one stitch of the previous round.

Instructions

Crocheting is a great way of moulding stitches to fit different vase shapes. For our vases shown here, we have used treble crochet throughout (pink vase) or 3 trebles and 1 raised treble alternately (white vase). To make the raised treble, instead of inserting the hook into the top of the stitch on the previous round as usual, pick up the whole treble crochet of the previous round. To do this, insert the hook from front to back, then through to the front again to the left of the treble crochet (see p.94).

The cover is worked from bottom to top. For all versions, work a foundation chain (see p.90) and join into a ring (see p.95). The length of the foundation chain should be the same as the circumference of the vase at the point where the vase cover should begin. All the trebles are then worked into this circle. As you work you can decrease or increase regularly, as required by the shape of the vase. Keep trying out the crochet work as you go along. Just before it is complete, pull the cover over the vase and work the final decreases.

The vase cover is stretchy enough to remove, for instance if you need to clean the vase.

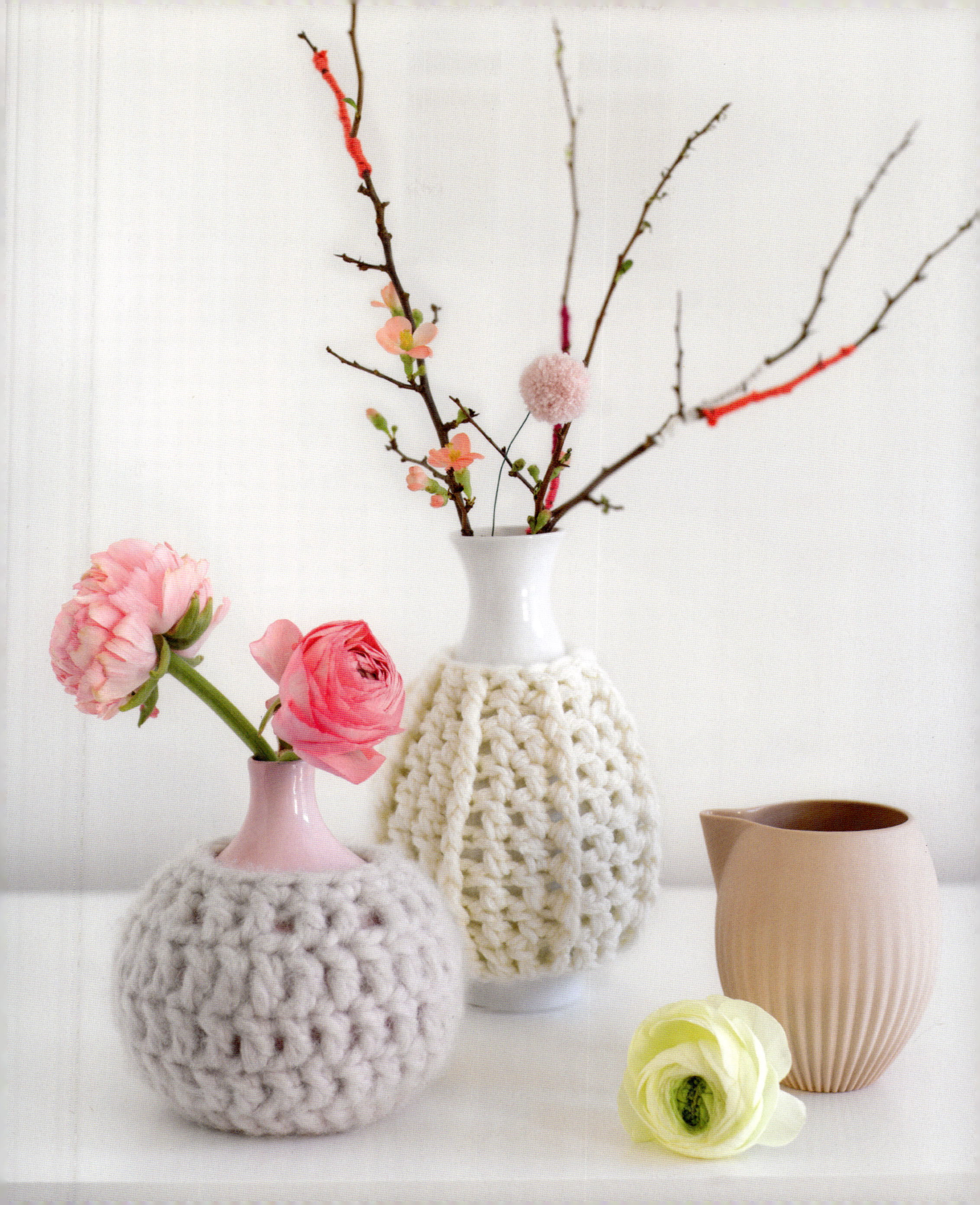

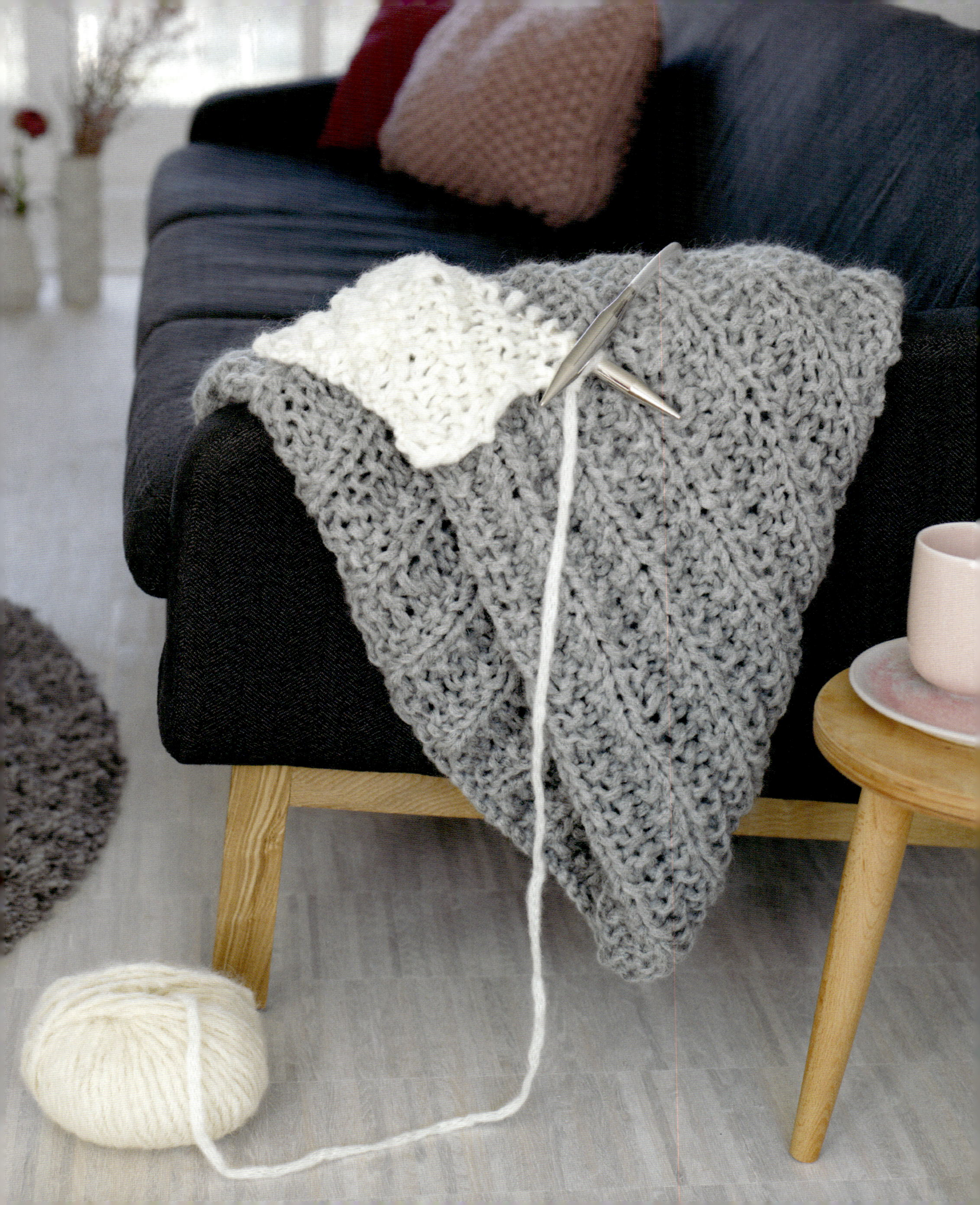

Cosy blanket

TIME 8 hours

Moderate

SIZE 1.2 × 1.2m (47 x 47in)

Materials

Yarn

Schachenmayr select Alegretto, 1000g in 08516 (silver)

Other items

15mm (US19) circular needle, 1m (39in) long

Instructions

To make this super-cosy but ultra-light blanket, cast on 102 stitches. Then, it's simply a case of working backwards and forwards in rows in this "mock fisherman's rib" pattern:

Row 1: [K3, p1] to last 2 sts, k2.
Row 2: [P1, k3] to last 2 sts, p1, k1.

Rep these 2 rows until you see the last ball coming to an end. Cast off.

Variation

Diagonal rib pattern: the number of stitches must be a multiple of 4. Work in rows backwards and forwards.

Row 1: [K2, p2] to end.
Row 2: K1, [p2, k2] to last 3 sts, p2, k1.
Row 3: [P2, k2] to end.
Row 4: P1, [k2, p2] to last 3 sts, k2, p1.
Rep rows 1–4 until the blanket is the size you want.

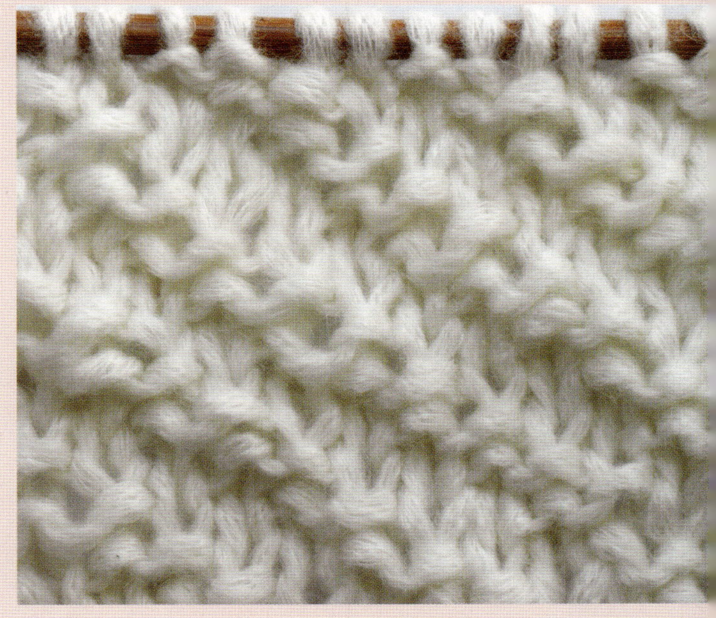

The diagonal rib pattern is great for a large cosy blanket: it is easy to knit and gives the blanket an interesting texture.

Pyramid door stops

TIME 1½–2 hours per door stop

Moderate

SIZE Side lengths 15cm and 20cm (6in and 8in)

Materials

Yarn for pink door stop

Schachenmayr select Apiretto, 50g in 08119 (powder)

Work with two strands of yarn.

Yarn for colour-graded door stop

Schachenmayr select Apiretto, 50g each of 08125 (white), 08119 (powder), and 08105 (lilac)

Work with two strands of yarn.

Other items

1 pair of 6mm (UK4/US10) needles

For the stuffing: 500–600g (1lb 2oz–1lb 5oz) rice, dried beans, or sand

Additional 50g (1¾oz) padding material for the large door stop

Light-coloured fabric remnant, approx. 30 x 15cm (12 x 6in) (pink door stop)

Light-coloured fabric remnant, approx. 40 x 20cm (16 x 8in) (colour-graded door stop)

Sewing machine (if available; otherwise sew by hand)

Matching thread

Instructions

For the pink door stop, cast on 40 stitches and work in garter stitch for 30 rows. For the colour-graded door stop, cast on 60 stitches and work 50 rows in garter stitch, changing yarn colour at regular intervals. Start with two white strands, change one strand after 12 rows to powder, and work 8 more rows. Then use the powder yarn for the second strand as well, and work another 10 rows. Finally swap a powder strand for a lilac one, work 8 rows, then change the second strand to lilac as well, and work another 12 rows.

The rectangular knitted pieces should make a square when folded down the middle. If not, adjust the number of rows given in the instructions either up or down.

Cast off, leaving a yarn tail approx. 40cm (16in) long. Measure the knitted piece to give the size for cutting the fabric inner, then fold the knitted rectangle in half to form a square. Carefully sew together the sides opposite the fold using mattress stitch (see p.89). Now, sew together one of the other open edges.

Cut the fabric remnant to the size of the knitted piece, adding a 1cm (½in) seam allowance on each side. Neaten all the edges with zigzag stitching. Fold into a square with right sides together, then join the sides opposite the fold using backstitch. Then, sew down one of the other open sides, as on the knitted piece.

To give the door stop its pyramidal shape, take the one remaining open side of the fabric inner and pull the two open edges together, opposite to the direction of the others, so that the seam on one edge meets the middle of the other edge. Sew together, leaving a small opening for the stuffing. Stuff with rice, beans, or sand, and padding material if used, and sew up the opening.

Put the filled fabric inner inside the knitted cover and give the cover the same pyramidal shape by matching the stitched seam on one open edge to the middle of the other open edge. Finally, graft the edges together.

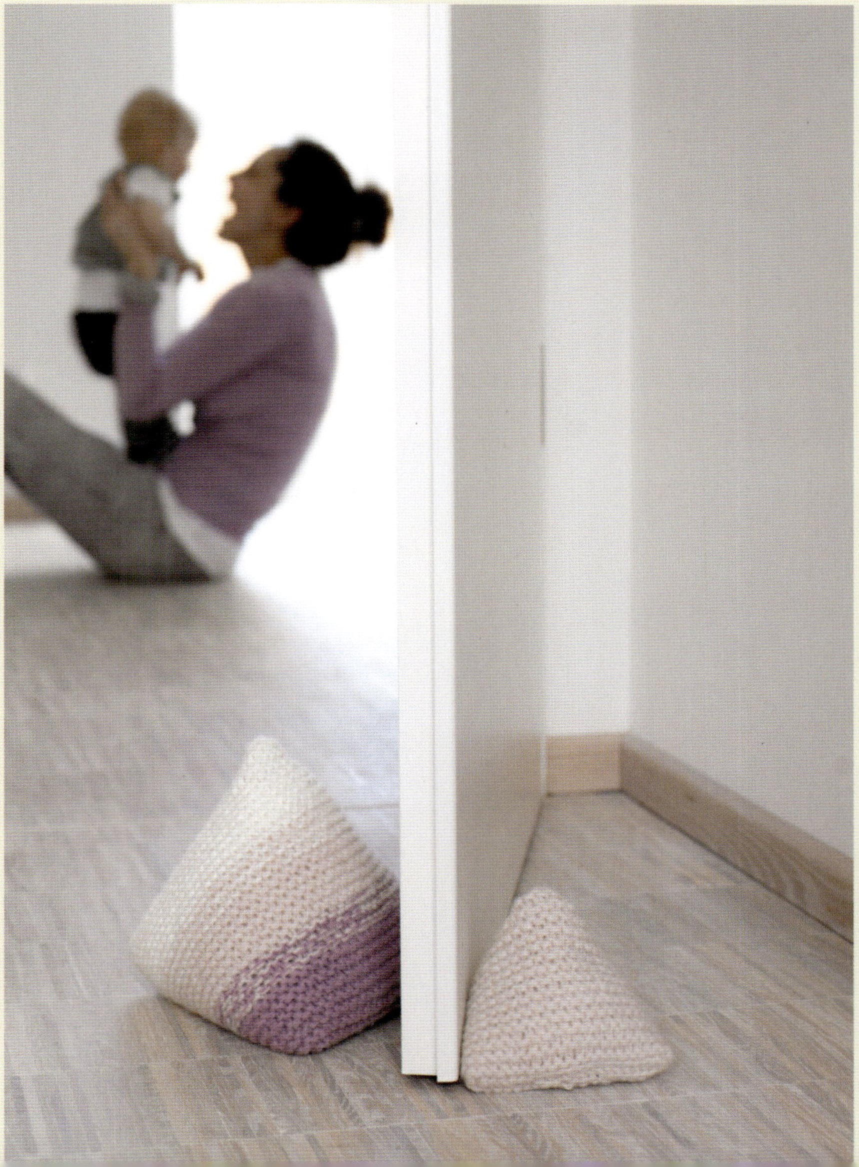

Variation

Creative knitters can experiment with colour grading when making this door stop, using more or fewer shades than those specified in the instructions and by changing colour at an earlier or later stage.

Stool cover

TIME 1 hour

Easy

SIZE Diameter of seat: 30cm (12in)

Materials

Yarn

Schachenmayr original Kadina Light, 200g in 00002 (natural)

Work with two strands of yarn.

Other items

12mm hook

Stool (shown here: IC-KUH "Buchholz milking stool").

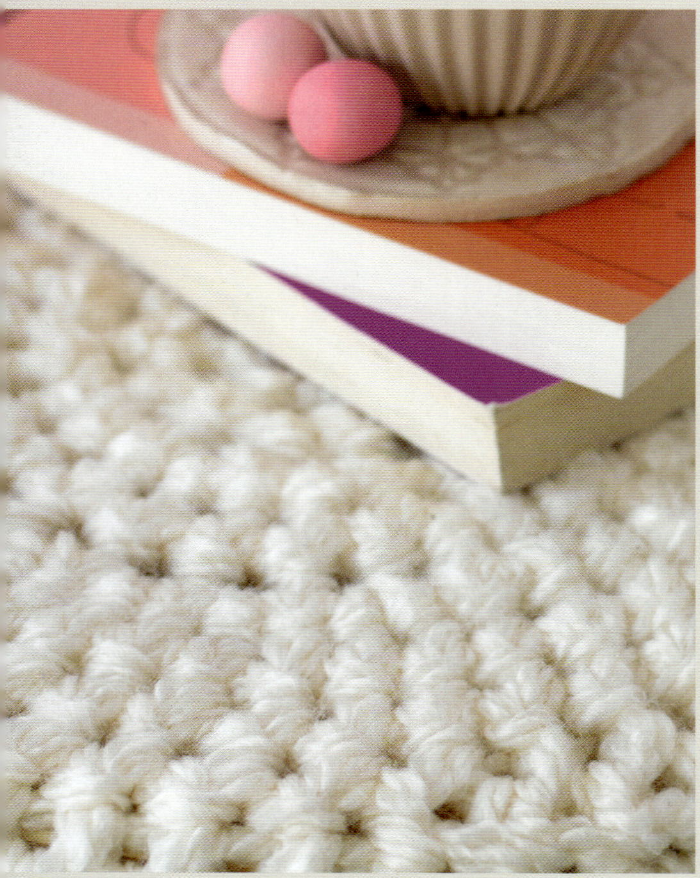

Instructions

Make a foundation ring (see p.95) of 6 dc.

Round 1: 2 dc in each dc (12 sts).
Round 2: 2 dc in each dc (24 sts).
Round 3: Dc.
Round 4: 2 dc in each dc (48 sts).
Rounds 5–7: Dc.
Rounds 8–10: Htr.

Fasten off by cutting the yarn and drawing it through the loop. Darn in the ends on the right side and pull the cover over the stool wrong side out. Then thread a long strand of yarn through the edge stitches with a blunt-ended needle and pull tight.

This cosy stool cover is crocheted in rounds from the centre outwards and tied in place under the seat with a strand of yarn.

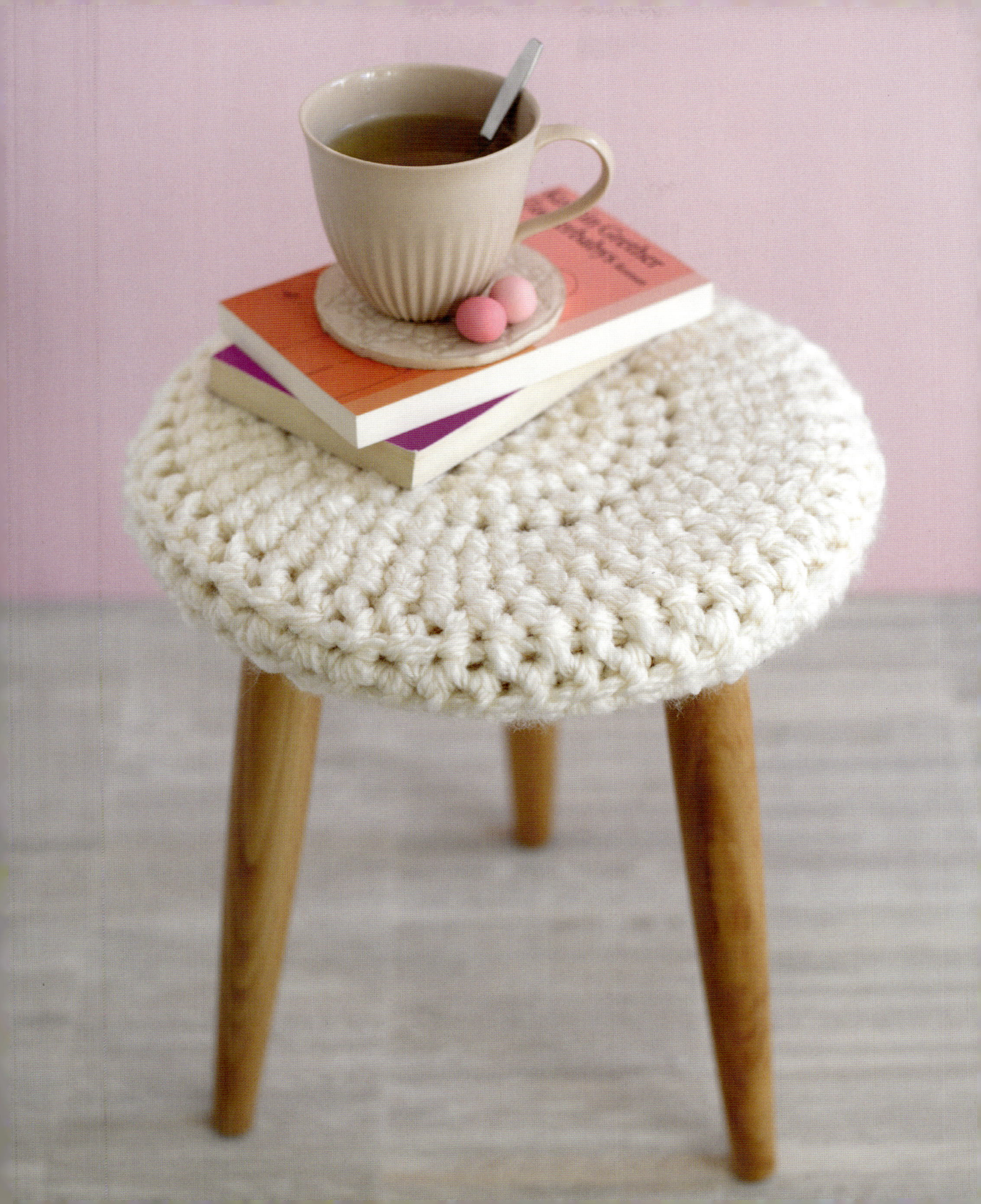

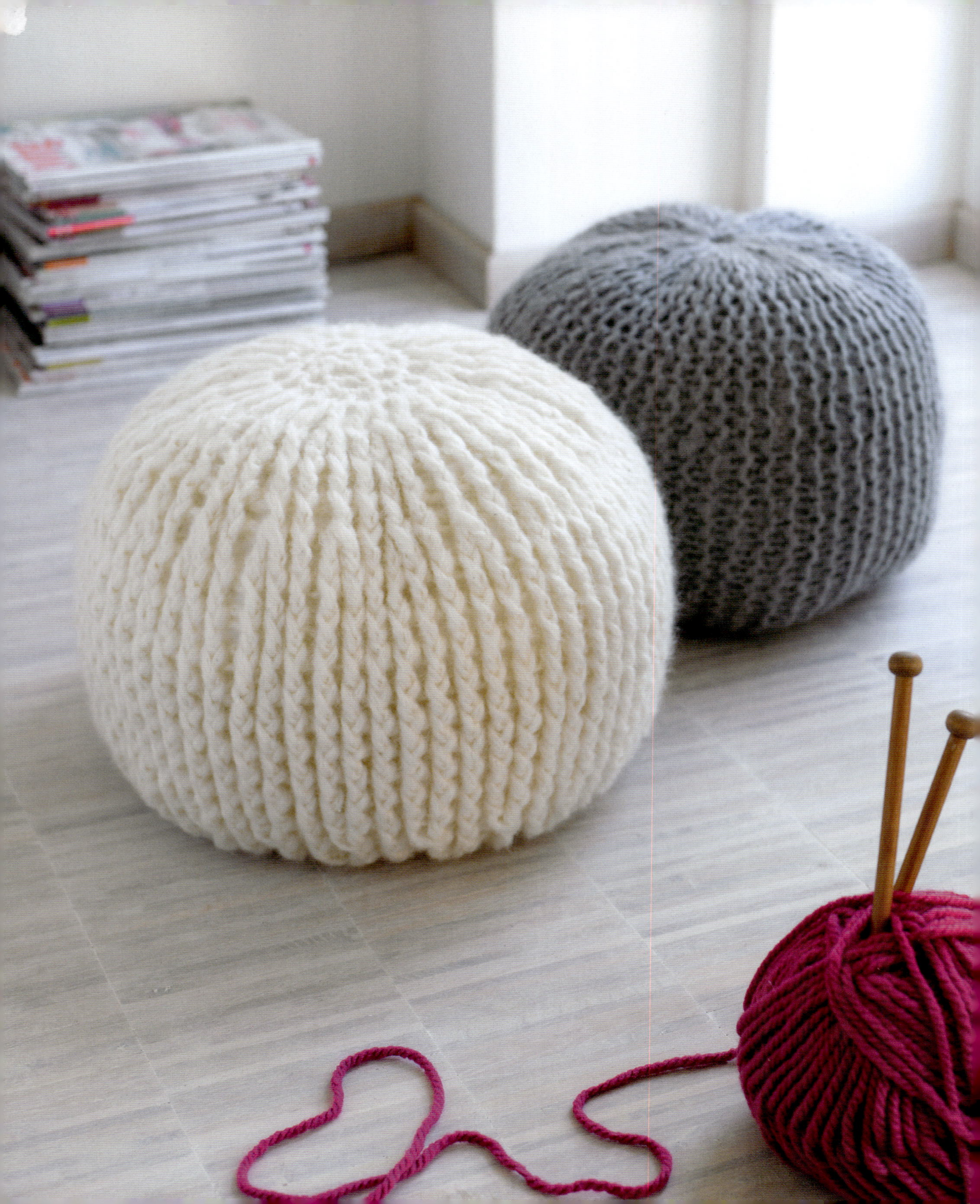

White crocheted pouffe

Materials

Yarn

Schachenmayr select Alegretto, 500g in 08525 (natural)

Other items

15mm hook

3 cushions for stuffing

TIME 5 hours

Moderate

SIZE Diameter 45cm (17¾in), height 35cm (13¾in)

Instructions

Remember to mark the first stitch of a round with a safety pin or stitch marker. Make a foundation ring (see p.95) of 4 dc.

Round 1: 2 dc in each dc (8 sts).
Round 2: 2 dc in each dc (16 sts).
Round 3: 2 tr in each dc (32 sts).
Round 4: Work 1 and 2 tr alternately in every st as RTRF (raised treble crochet front: see p.94) (48 sts).
Rounds 5–6: RTRF.
Round 7: Alt 1 and 2 tr in every st as RTRF (72 sts).
Rounds 8–15: RTRF.
Round 16: Alt 1 RTRF and tr2tog (see Treble decrease, p.95) (48 sts).
Round 17: RTRF.
Round 18: As round 16 (32 sts).
Round 19: As round 17.
Round 20: Tr2tog (16 sts).
Round 21: Tr.
Stuff the pouffe with the cushions.
Round 22: Tr2tog (8 sts).
Round 23: Tr.
Rep rounds 22 and 23 until the pouffe is almost closed. Then draw the yarn through the last stitches and pull tight.

Grey knitted pouffe

Materials

Yarn

Schachenmayr select Alegretto, 400g in 08516 (silver)

Other items

12mm (US17) circular needle, 80cm (32in) long
3 cushions for stuffing

TIME 3½ hours

Moderate

SIZE Diameter 35cm (13¾in), height 30cm (12in)

Instructions

Cast on 28 stitches using the provisional method (see p.86). Knit 125 rows in garter stitch. Do not cast off; cut the yarn, leaving a tail approx. 70cm (27½in) long.

Graft the cast-on and cast-off edges of the work together to form a ring using Kitchener stitch (see below). Then draw the yarn through the side edge, pull tight, and fasten off.

Stuff the pouffe with the cushions and pull the other edge together with a strand of yarn.

How to do Kitchener stitch

Pick up the first row you knitted onto a needle. The contrasting yarn used for the provisional cast-on makes this easier, but remove it once you have finished picking up. Place the two knitting needles side by side with right sides outwards and the working yarn coming from the rear needle. Thread the yarn through a blunt-ended needle.

Insert the needle and yarn purlwise through the first stitch on the front needle. Then insert it knitwise into the first stitch of the rear needle and pull the yarn through. The following four steps are then repeated to the end:

1. Insert the threaded needle knitwise into the first stitch of the front knitting needle and slip the stitch off the needle.

2. From the back, insert the threaded needle purlwise into the next stitch on the front knitting needle and pull through, leaving the stitch on the needle.

3. From the back, insert the threaded needle purlwise into the first stitch of the rear knitting needle and slip the stitch off the needle.

4. From the front, insert the threaded needle knitwise into the next stitch on the rear knitting needle and pull through, leaving the stitch on the needle.

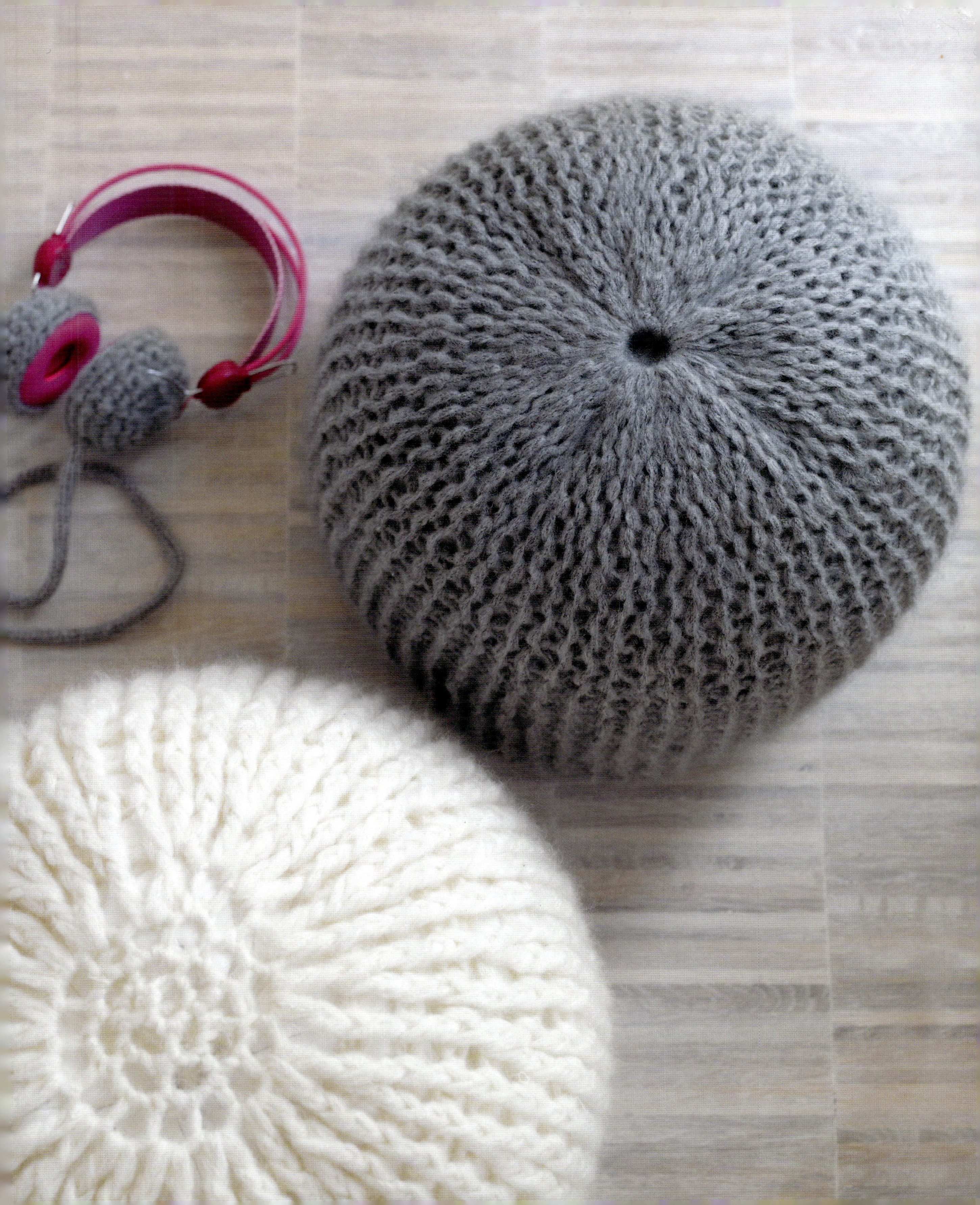

Cat house

TIME 4 hours

Easy knitting, but requires good craft skills

SIZE Height 45cm (17¾in)

Materials

Yarn

Schachenmayr select Alegretto, 350g in 08516 (silver)

Other items

1 pair of 15mm (US19) needles

Tension wire, approx. 3mm (⅛in) diameter (from DIY or craft stores)

Cable ties

Pliers

Instructions

Following the diagram (see right) bend the wire into shape to make the frame for the cat house, joining it together with cable ties. Snip off any cable tie ends close to the wire, with the pliers, so that the cat does not get injured.

The cat house is made up of two knitted pieces: the back wall and a long central piece that forms the roof, sides, and floor. The basic pattern is quite simple: knit 1 row, purl 1 row, and repeat (stocking stitch).

To make the central piece, cast on 24 stitches. Work approx. 115 rows in stocking stitch. The knitted piece must fit tightly on the frame.
Cast off.

For the back wall, cast on 16 stitches. Work approx. 24 rows in stocking stitch, then start to decrease: on every knit row: K1, s1, k1, psso, knit until 3 sts remain, k2tog, k1.
Next row: Purl.
Rep until you reach the roof ridge.

Fit the central piece around the wire frame and graft the ends together along the roof ridge (see p.89). Then sew the back wall onto the frame and the edges of the central piece.

Start by bending the wire into shape to make two back and front sections, two side sections, and a roof ridge.

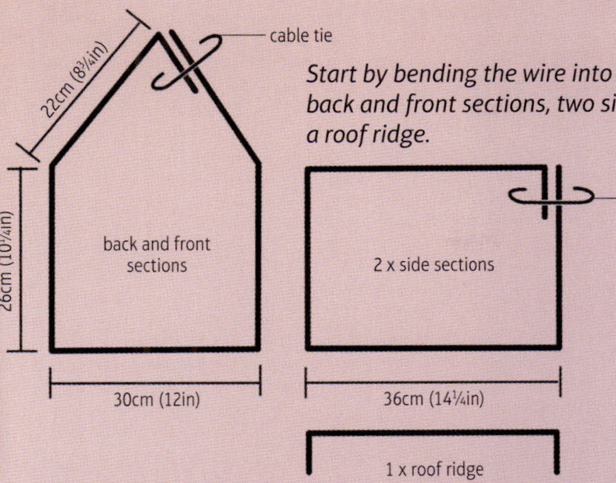

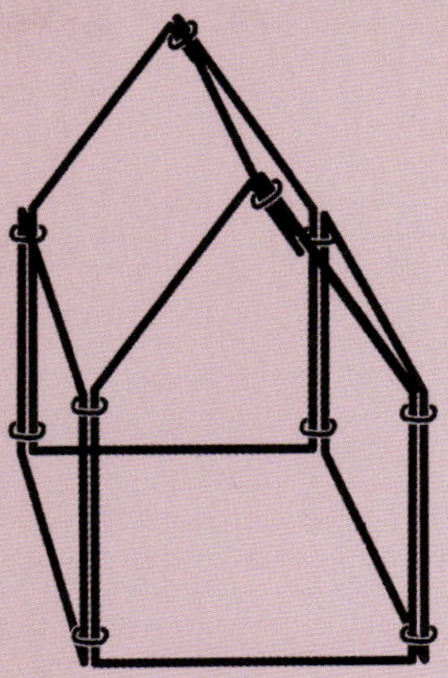

Join the five wire sections together with cable ties (as shown above) to make a house.

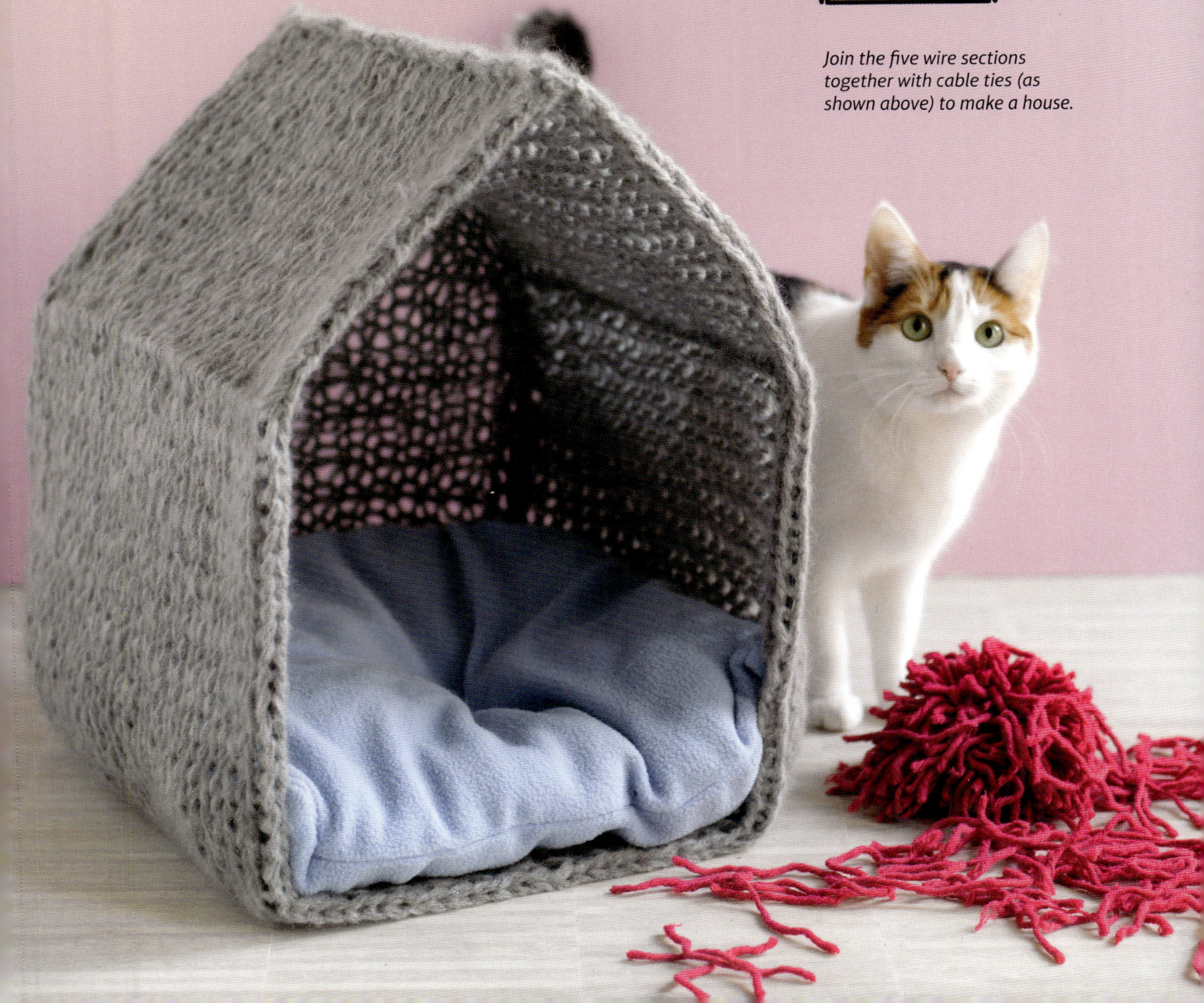

Tablet and headphones covers

Tablet cover

TIME 1 hour

Easy

SIZE 24 × 18.5cm (9½ x 7¼in)

Headphones cover

TIME 2 hours

Easy

SIZE To fit all headphones

Materials

Yarn for tablet cover

Schachenmayr original Bravo Big, 200g in 00102 (natural)

Work with two strands of yarn.

Yarn for headphones cover

Schachenmayr original Bravo, 50g each in 08234 (neon pink) and 08295 (medium grey heather)

Other items for tablet cover

15mm hook

Other items for headphones cover

10mm hook

Knitting mill or French knitter

Headphones with removable speakers

Instructions for tablet cover

The size of the protective cover can be adjusted. The length of the foundation chain is determined by the width of the tablet. In this version, the foundation chain has 18 stitches.

The cover is worked entirely in double crochet. This means you start with the second stitch from the hook and work double crochet along the chain. At the end of the chain, simply turn the work through 180° and work back along the other side of the chain. Then start with the first double crochet of the previous row. Continue working in rows.

To produce this very thick stitch pattern, insert the hook between the vertical strands directly under the stitch instead of between its two loops. So, you insert the hook directly into the middle, the “V” of the stitch on the previous row. Repeat until the cover fits the tablet.

Fasten off with a slip stitch on the previous row and weave in the yarn.

Instructions for headphones cover

Remove the two headphones from the headband. Work double crochet in rounds with double strands. Start by working 6 double crochets into a foundation ring (see p.95). In the next round, work 2 double crochets in each stitch. In the following rounds, increase only in every second stitch. When the piece is the right diameter to fit the headphone, work a few

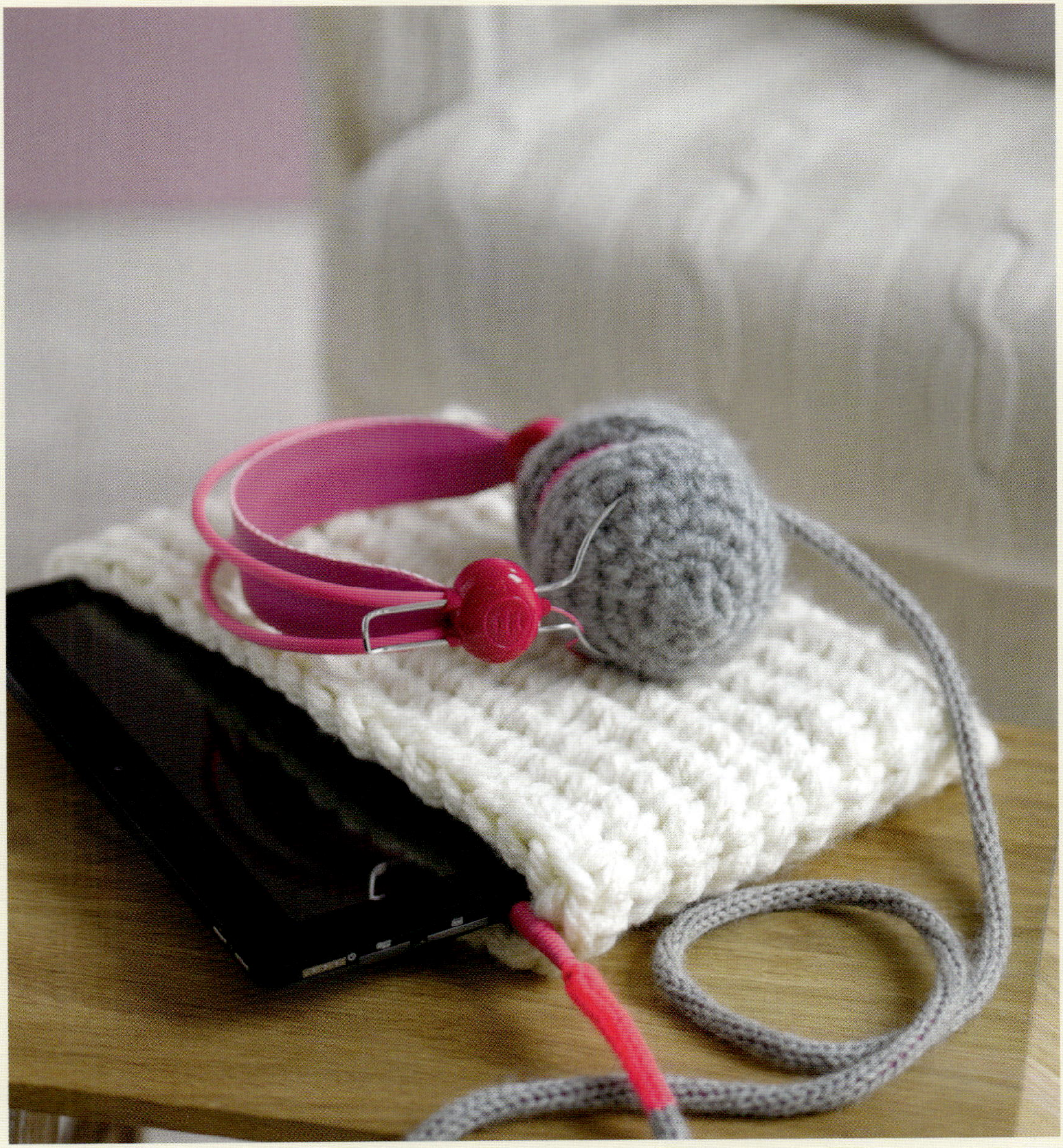

rounds straight, checking the shape as you go. Remember to work round the cable. Fasten off and pull the cover over the headphones, then re-attach them.

To make the cable cover, work a tube with a knitting mill or French knitter. Make it the same length as the cable and change colours as desired. Leave the end of the tube open and carefully feed the cable through it. Once the cable is through, pull the end together and fasten with a knot. The only part left uncovered and visible is the jack plug.

Textural cushion cover

Materials

Yarn

Rowan Big Wool, 500g in 00064 (Prize)
Work with two strands of yarn.

Other items

1 pair of 15mm (US19) needles
Cushion pad measuring 35 x 50cm (14 x 20in)

TIME 3 hours

Easy

SIZE 35 × 50cm
(14 x 20in)

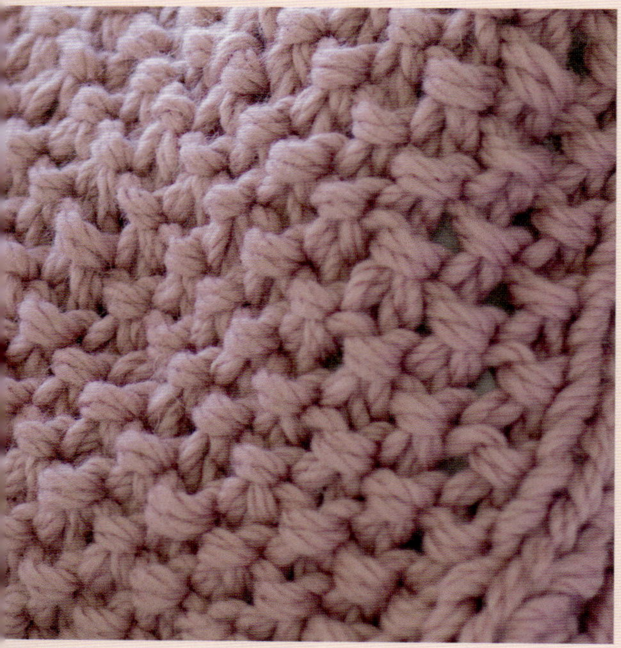

The simple moss stitch used for this cushion cover gives a thick, dense texture when combined with the double-stranded yarn.

Instructions

For the front of the cushion cover, cast on 32 stitches. From row 3 onwards the pattern you'll be knitting is known as moss stitch.

Row 1: P.
Row 2: K.
Row 3: P2, [p1, k1] to last 2 sts, p2.
Row 4: K2, [k1, p1] to last 2 sts, k2. Rep rows 3 and 4 15 times.
Last row: Cast off.

Work the back of the cover as for the front. Join the two pieces together with mattress stitch (see p.89), leaving a 20cm (8in) opening for stuffing. Insert the cushion pad and then sew up the opening to finish off.

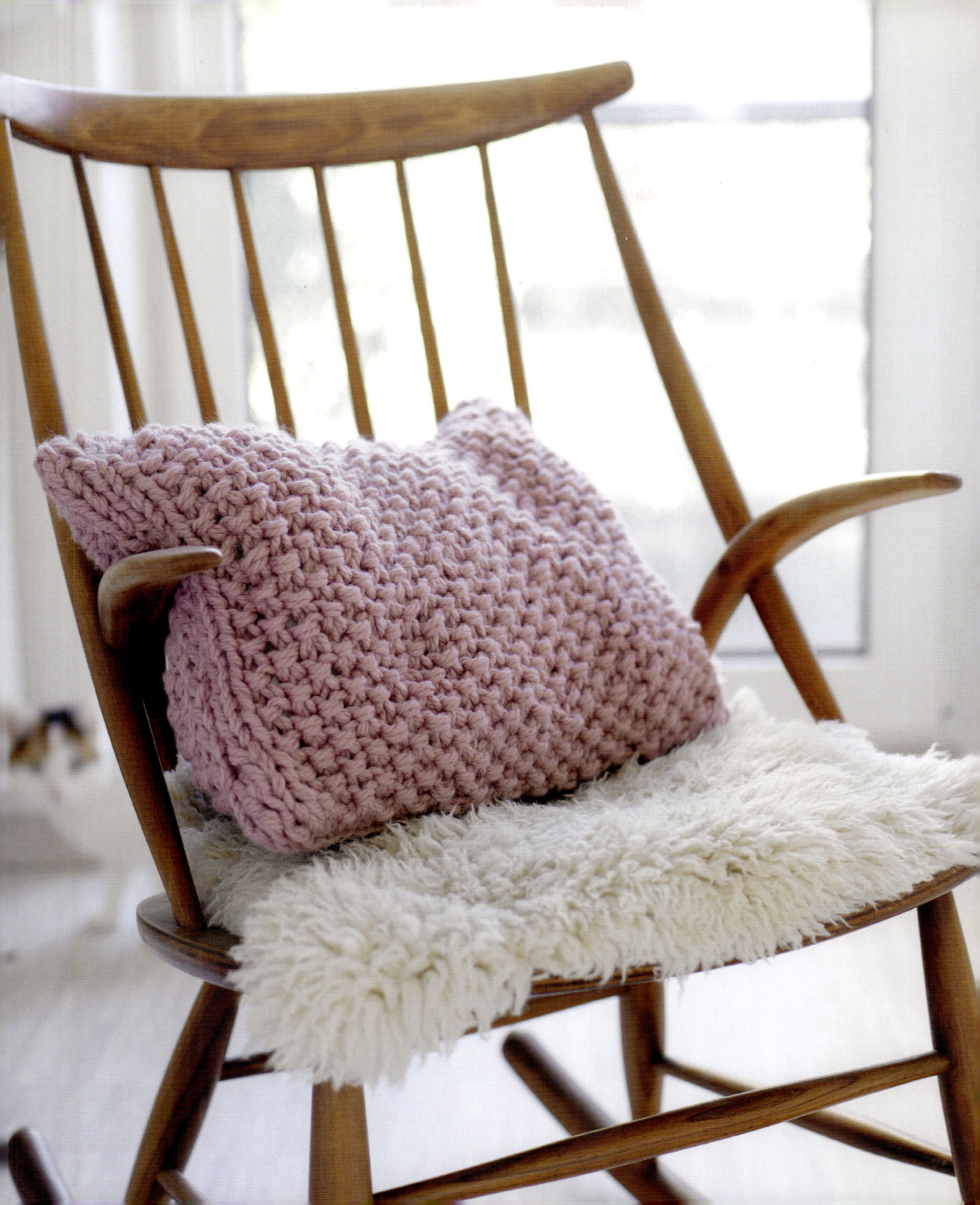

Decorative hearts

TIME 40 minutes per heart

Moderate

SIZE 9 × 10cm (3½ x 4in)

Materials

Yarn

Schachenmayr original Merino Super Big Mix, 100g makes at least 6 hearts, in 00090 (stone grey) and 00036 (cardinal)

Other items

1 pair of 5mm (UK6/US8) needles
Polyester soft toy stuffing

Instructions

Start at the tip of the heart. Cast on 2 stitches.

Row 1: Make 1 stitch by inserting the needle knitwise into the back of the first stitch, without slipping it off the left needle. With the yarn at the back, knit into the front of the first stitch and slip it off (= M1). Repeat on the second stitch.

Row 2: P.
Row 3: M1 (as described above), k to last st, M1 (6 sts).
Row 4: P.
Rows 5–12: Rep rows 3 and 4 until you have 14 sts on the needle.

Heart's right curve

Row 13: K2tog, k5, turn, leave rem 7 sts on a spare needle.
Row 14: P2tog, p2, p2tog (4 sts).
Row 15: Cast off rem 4 sts, and cut yarn, leaving a tail approx. 50cm (20in) long. Thread the tail through the edge to the centre of the heart.

Heart's left curve

Return to rem 7 sts and work with the 50cm (20in) yarn tail.
Row 13: K5, k2tog.
Row 14: P2tog, p2, p2tog.
Row 15: Cast off rem 4 sts.

Make another heart in the same way. Sew the two hearts together with mattress stitch (see p.89), leaving a small opening. Stuff the heart with the filling material and close up.

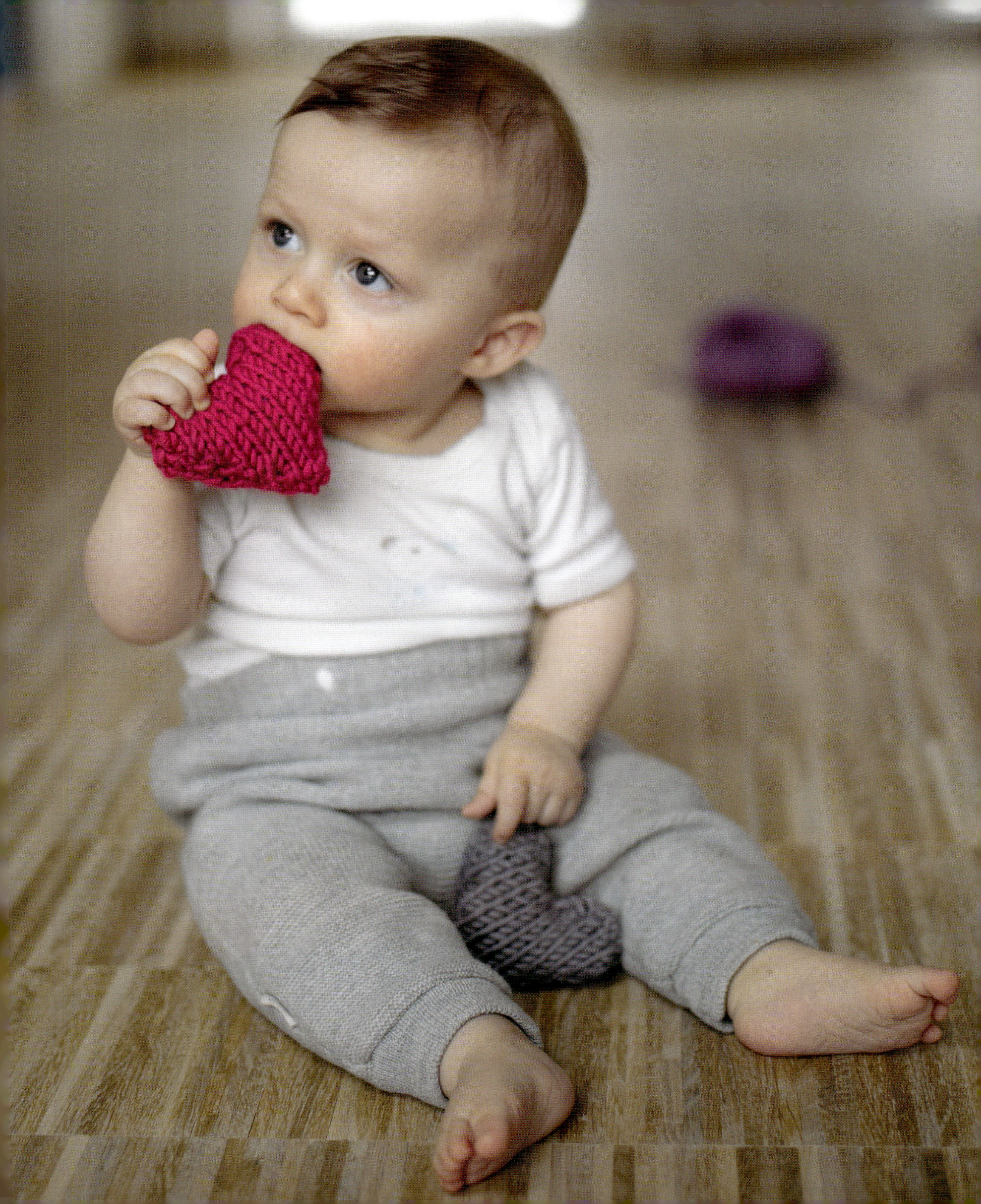

Dog basket

TIME 4 hours

Easy

SIZE Diameter 50cm (20in)

Materials

Yarn for dog basket
Schachenmayr original Aventica, 300g in 00090 (grey mix)
Work with two strands of yarn.

Yarn for dog bone
Schachenmayr original Boston, 50g in 00002 (natural)

Other items for dog basket
9mm hook
Polyester soft toy stuffing

Other items for dog bone
7mm hook
Polyester soft toy stuffing

Instructions for dog basket

This item is crocheted in rounds from the centre out. Start the item off by making a foundation ring (see p.95) with 6 dc.

Round 1: 2 htr in every dc (12 st).
Round 2: 2 htr in every dc (24 sts). After this row, always insert the hook under the back loop only, instead of both loops. This creates a nice pattern.
Round 3: 2 htr in every st (48 sts).
Rounds 4–5: Htr in every st.
Round 6: 1 and 2 htr alternately (72 sts).
Rounds 7–8: Htr.
Round 9: 1 and 2 htr alternately (108 sts).
Round 10: Htr.
Round 11: Htr, with 2 htr in every third st (144 sts).

Continue working in half trebles for 15cm (6in). Fold the border outwards and sew it to the base of the basket to create a ring around the edge. Leave a small opening for the filling. Stuff the filling into the ring and sew it closed.

Instructions for dog bone

Who could resist crocheting this cute little bone?
Round 1: 2 ch, work 6 dc in second chain.
Round 2: 2 dc in each stitch (12 sts).
Rounds 3–4: Work in dc, fasten off with slip stitch in first stitch of the row.

Make a second piece in the same way. Attach the two pieces together with 2 dc. Work dc round both pieces, and at the two points where the pieces meet work dc2tog (4 sts fewer). Work 2 more rows in this way (8 sts fewer). Now work 8 rows dc. Make the second half of the bone in the same way, stuff both pieces with the stuffing material, and sew together.

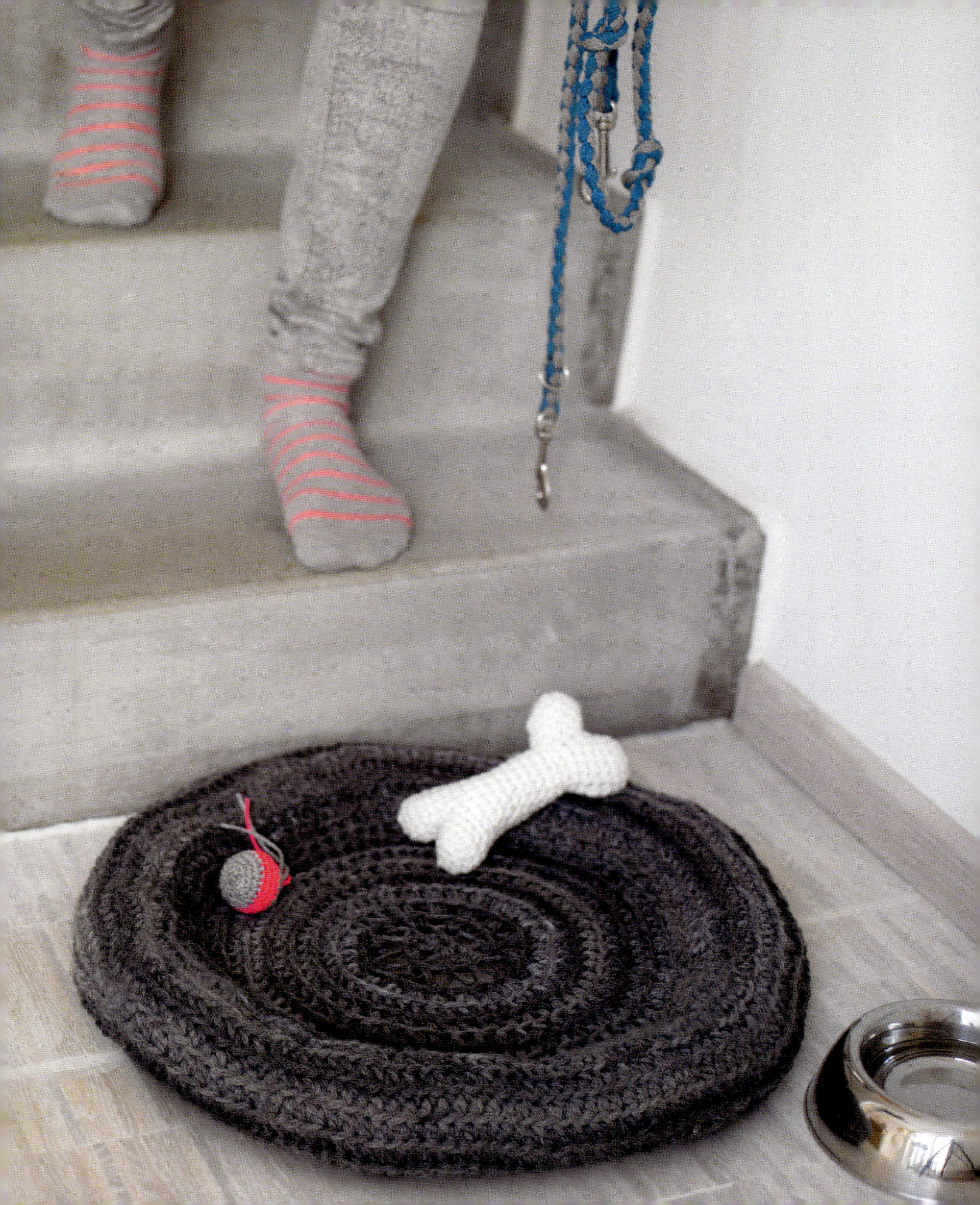

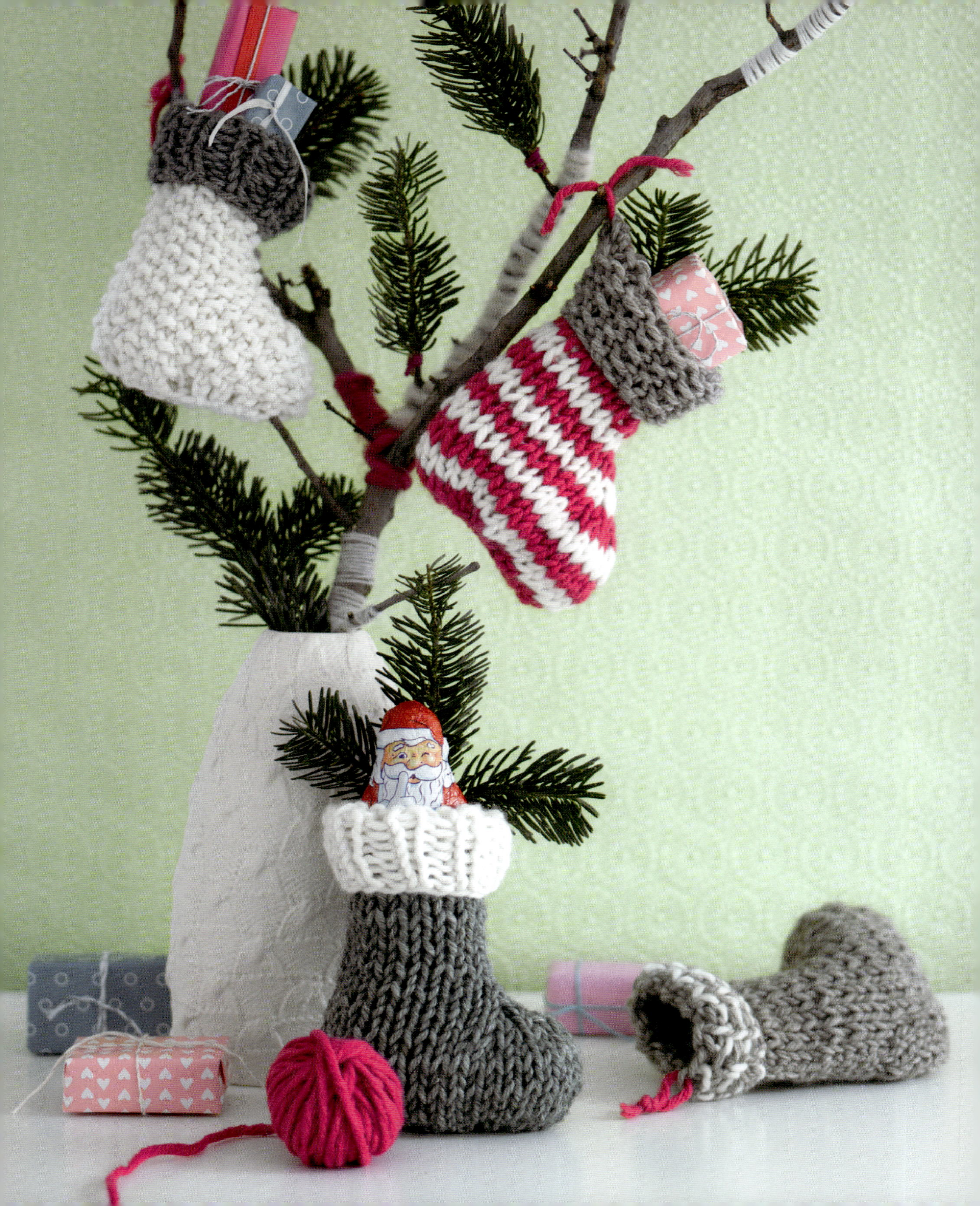

Mini Christmas stockings

TIME 45 minutes per stocking

Moderate

SIZE Height 18cm (7in), width 7–13cm (2¾–5¼in)

Materials

Yarn

Schachenmayr original Boston, 50g each of 00092 (mid grey), 00002 (natural), and 00035 (pink)

Other items

1 pair of 8mm (UK0/US11) needles

Instructions

These woolly items are knitted in rows in stocking stitch. Cast on 16 stitches.

Row 1: P.
Row 2: *K1, make 1 by picking up and knitting the horizontal strand between the stitches (= M1L, see p.88), repeat from * to last st, k1 (31 sts).
Row 3: P.
Row 4: K.
Rows 5–8: Rep rows 3–4 twice more.
Row 9: P.
Row 10: K8, k2tog x 3, k3tog, k2tog x 3, k8 (23 sts).
Row 11: P.
Row 12: K8, k2tog, k3tog, k2tog, k8 (19 sts).
Row 13: P.
Row 14: K8, k3tog, k8 (17 sts).
Row 15: P.
Row 16: K.
Rows 17–22: Rep rows 15–16 three times.
Row 23: P (17 sts).

The next section is the top cuff, so change the colour here if you like.
Row 24: P.
Row 25: K.
Rows 26–28: P.

The next 6 rows are worked in pattern for the cuff, either in ordinary rib (right side [k1, p1] to last st, k1; and wrong side [p1, k1] to last st, p1; or in moss stitch (every row [k1, p1] to last st, k1) (see p.30).

Cast off, and sew the seam from the top down in mattress stitch (see p.89).

Variation

Make the stripy version by changing the yarn colour every second row from row 5. You can, of course, do the whole stocking in moss stitch or garter stitch: the increases and decreases remain the same.

Cloud cushions

TIME 2 hours per cushion

Moderate

SIZE 40 × 23cm (16 x 9in), 25 × 12cm (9¾ x 5in)

Materials

Yarn

Rowan Alpaca Chunky, 200g in 072 (wren)

Other items

1 pair of 12mm (US17) needles
Polyester soft toy stuffing

Instructions

The cushions are worked in garter stitch, that is knitting every row. Cast on 30 stitches.

Row 1: K.
Row 2: K1, make 1 by picking up and knitting the horizontal strand between the stitches (= M1L, see p.88), knit to last 2 sts, k1, M1L, k1 (32 sts).
Row 3: K.
Rows 4–9: Rep rows 2 and 3 three times (38 sts).
Rows 10–13: K.
Row 14: K1, s1, k1, psso, k to end (37 sts).
Row 15: K.
Rows 16–19: Rep rows 14 and 15 twice (35 sts).
Row 20: S1, k1, psso, k1, pass last st over, k1, pass last st over, k1, pass last st over, k until only 3 sts rem on left needle, k2tog, k1 (30 sts).
Row 21: K.
Row 22: K until only 3 sts rem on left needle, k2tog, k1 (29 sts).
Row 23: K.
Row 24: As row 22 (28 sts).
Row 25: K.
Row 26: As row 22 (27 sts).
Row 27: S1, k1, psso, k1, pass last st over, k1, pass last st over, knit to end (24 sts).
Row 28: K1, s1, k1, psso, k until 3 sts rem on left needle, k2tog, k1 (22 sts).
Row 29: K.
Rows 30–33: Rep rows 28 and 29 twice (18 sts).
Row 34: S1, k1, psso, k1, pass last st over, k1, pass last st over, k1, pass last st over, k until only 3 sts rem on needle, k2tog, k1 (13 sts).
Row 35: K.
Row 36: K1, s1, k1, psso, k until 3 sts rem on needle, k2tog, k1 (11 sts).
Row 37: K.
Row 38: As row 36 (9 sts).
Row 39: K.
Row 40: As row 36 (7 sts).

Row 41: S1, k1, psso, k1, pass last st over.
Continue in the same way until every st has been cast off.
Knit two of these clouds. Lay the pieces on top of each other and graft together carefully (see p.89), leaving an opening for the stuffing. Put the stuffing inside and sew it closed.

Variation

The white cloud is made with Schachenmayr select Apiretto, 08125 (white), using size 6mm (UK4/US10) needles. The instructions are as for the grey cloud.

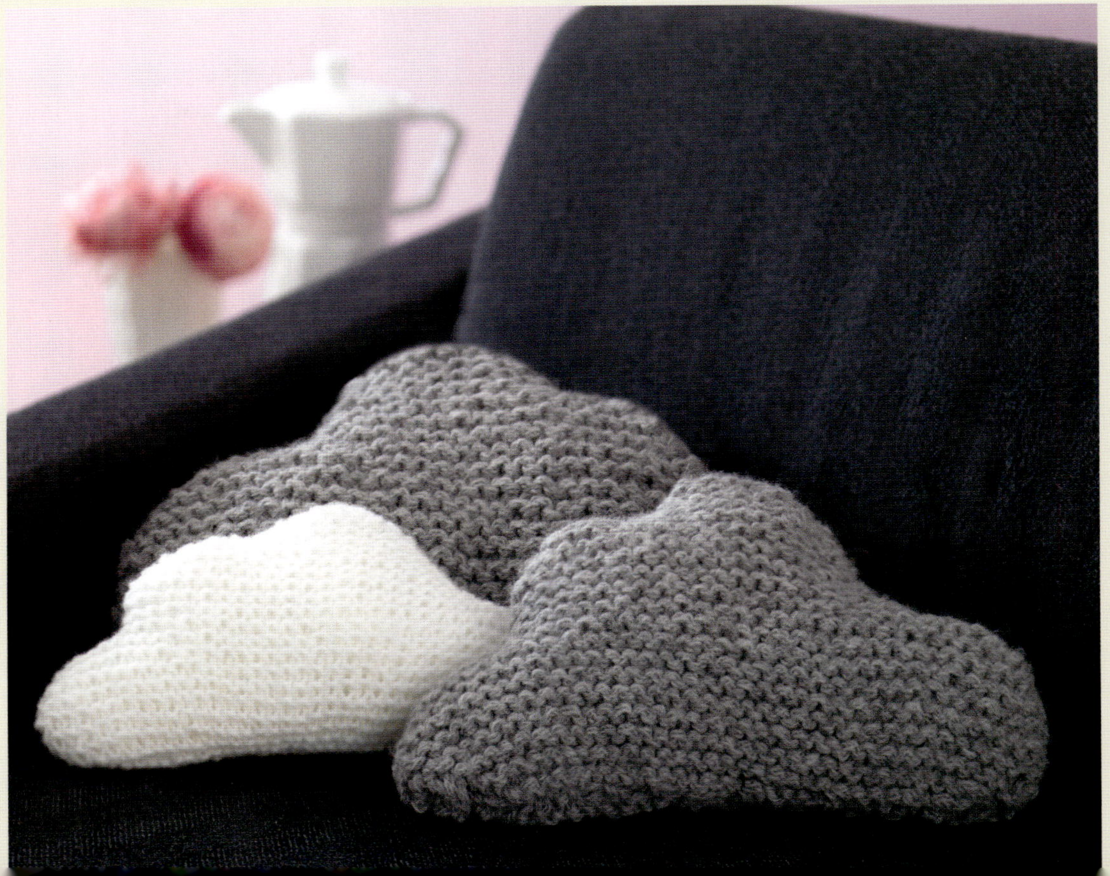

Lampshade

TIME Approx 1½ hours

Easy

SIZE Diameter 23cm (9in), height 16.5cm (6½in)

Materials

Yarn

Schachenmayr select Alegretto, 50g in 08525 (natural) and Schachenmayr select Highland Alpaca, 100g in 02925 (cream)

Other items

10mm (UK000/US15) and 12mm (US17) circular needles, 60cm (23½in) long
Lampshade (shown here: IKEA "Jära")

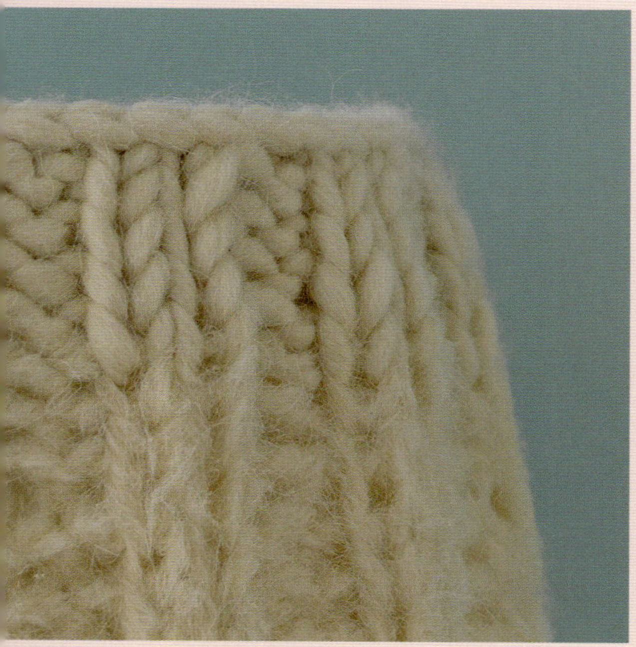

The tapered shape is achieved by changing the yarn and needle size, while maintaining the rib pattern.

Instructions

Cast on 52 stitches and join to work in the round. Here you'll use a simple k2, p2 rib.

Begin with 12mm (US17) needles and Alegretto yarn, working three-quarters of the height of the lampshade in rounds. Keep checking the knitted piece against the item to make sure you have reached the correct height.

Change the needles and the yarn, working the remaining quarter with Highland Alpaca and the 10mm (UK000/US15) needles. Cast off.

Pull the work over the lampshade. Draw a strand of yarn through the bottom edge, and tighten the cover slightly.

Variation

If your lampshade is a different size, but has a similar basic shape, the first thing to do is knit a tension sample in the rib described above. Then measure the lampshade, apply the tension results to the new size, and cast on the required number of stitches (in a multiple of 4).

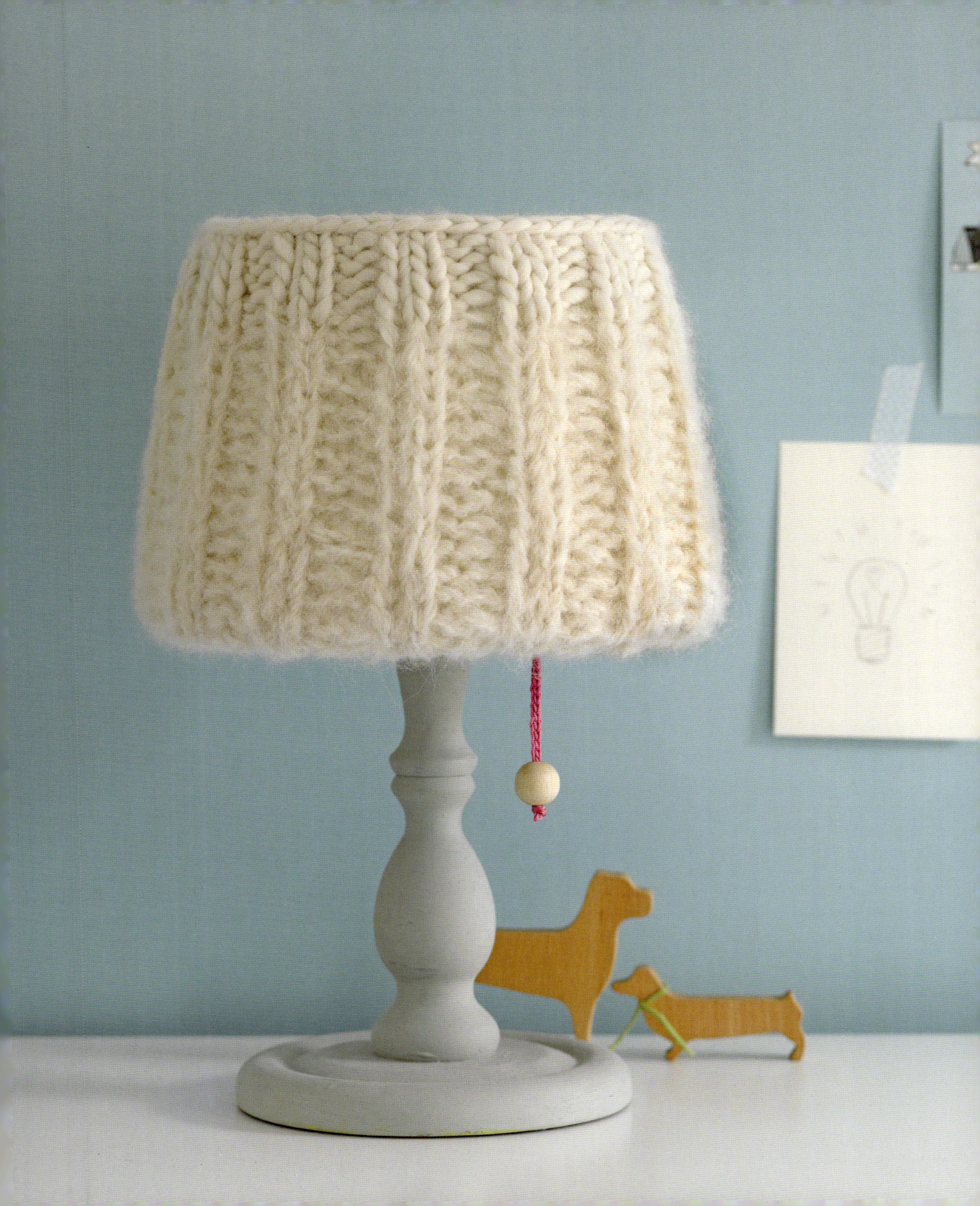

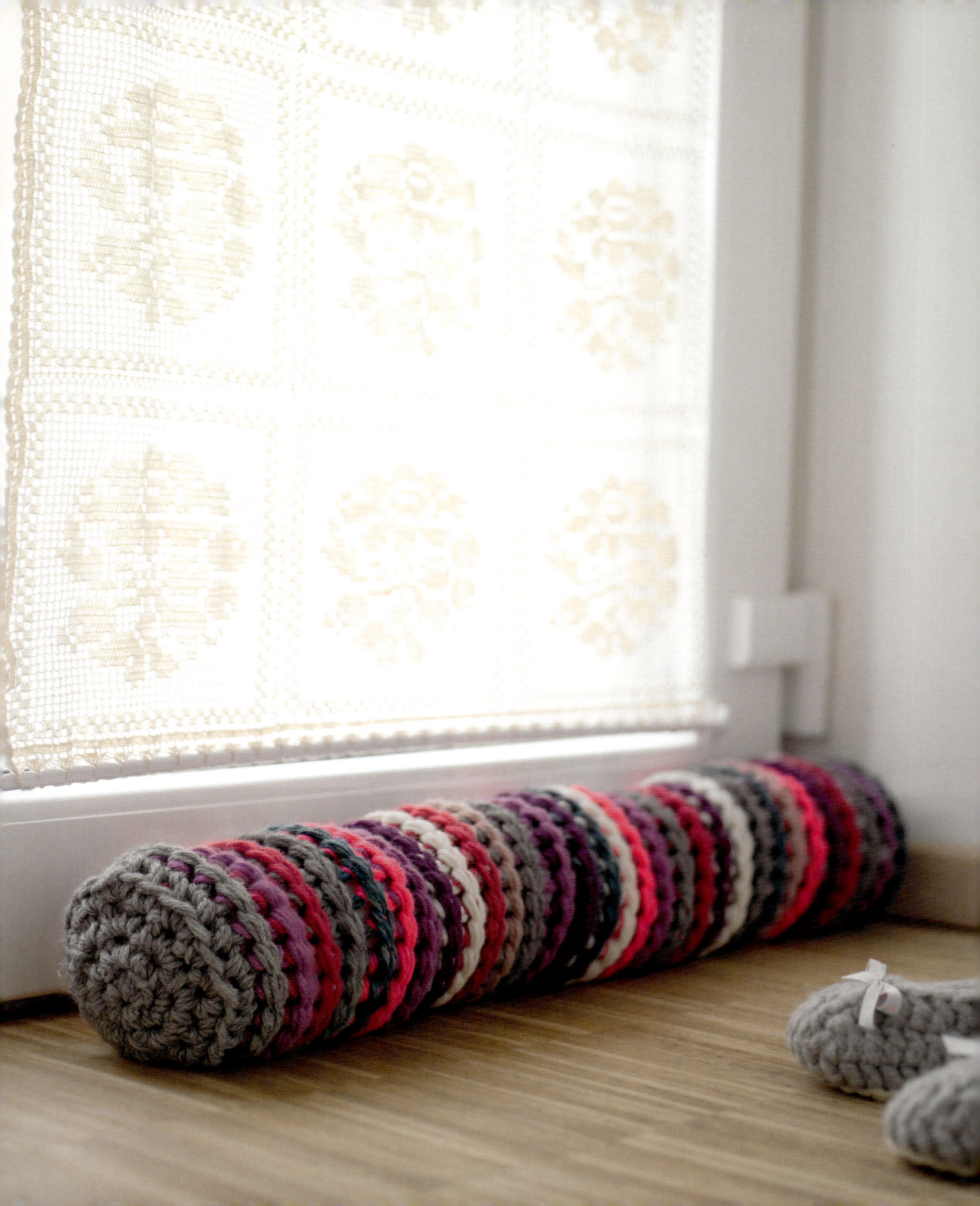

Draught excluder

TIME 1½ hours

Easy

SIZE Diameter 14cm (5½in); adjust the length to fit the door

Materials

Yarn

Schachenmayr original Boston, 50g each in 00002 (natural), 00136 (neon pink), 00047 (lavender), 00035 (pink), 00049 (violet), 00281 (casual marl), and 00092 (mid grey)

Work with two strands of yarn.

Other items

15mm hook

Polyester soft toy stuffing

Instructions

In a foundation ring (see p.95) work 4 dc. Continue to crochet the work in rounds.

Round 1: 2 dc in each st (8 sts).
Round 2: 2 dc in each st (16 sts).
Round 3: Alternate 1 and 2 dc in each st (24 sts).
Round 4: Dc, but only insert hook into back loop.

For the following rounds: work htr as RTRB (see p.94), that is around the htr of the previous row, changing the yarn colour after each round.

When the draught excluder is long enough, work 1 round in dc. Then decrease as follows:
3rd last round: [Dc, dc 2tog] to end; see Double crochet decrease, p.95 (16 sts).
2nd last round: Dc2tog to end (8 sts).
Last round: Dc2tog to end (4 sts).
Stuff the draught excluder with the stuffing and draw the yarn through the remaining stitches. Pull together tightly and weave in the end.

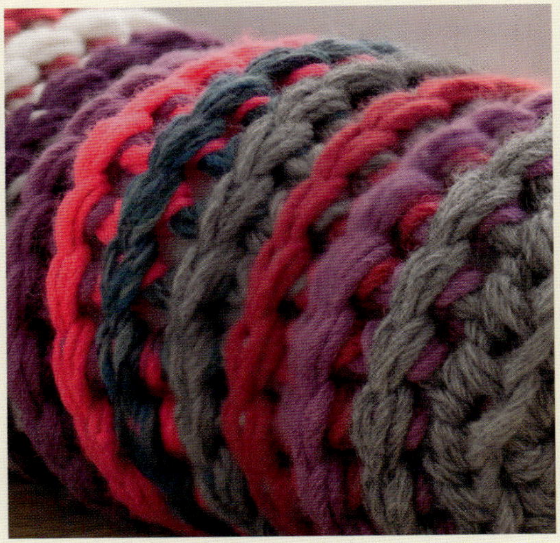

The raised trebles give a ring-like, sculptured texture.

Cute pussycat

TIME 1½ hours

Moderate

SIZE 25 × 22cm (9¾ x 8¾in), plus legs

Materials

Yarn

Schachenmayr original Bravo Big, 200g each in 00102 (natural) and 00110 (taupe)

Other items

8mm (UK0/US11) circular needle, 40cm (16in) long
4 x 8mm (UK0/US11) double-pointed needles
Buttons and contrasting yarn for the face
Polyester soft toy stuffing

Instructions

Cast on 40 stitches with the circular needle. The basic pattern is stocking stitch. Work 20 rows in st st with the natural-coloured yarn.

Continue in the basic pattern:
[2 rows taupe, 2 rows natural] twice, turn, cast off the first 5 sts with taupe yarn.

Now start the first leg, which is knitted in the round with 4 needles. Place the next 4 sts on the first needle, 3 sts on the second needle, and 3 sts on the third needle. Knit 10 rows on these 10 sts, alternating taupe and natural yarns. Knit 5 more rows in natural.

Graft the opening at the bottom of the leg together with Kitchener stitch (see p.24). Divide the stitches onto two needles. Hold them parallel, with the yarn coming from the back needle. Cut the yarn, leaving a 50cm (20in) tail, and thread it into a blunt-ended needle. Graft the 2 rows of stitches together as on page 24.

Once the first leg is complete, continue along the bottom edge of the body. In taupe, cast off the next 10 sts from the circular needle, k10, and cast off the last 5 sts.

For the second leg, work on the remaining 10 sts as for the first leg.

Join the back seam of the cat invisibly with mattress stitch (see p.89). Graft the top seam together (see p.89). Stuff the cat to a suitable plumpness and graft the bottom seam. Sew on the nose, cheeks, mouth, and various buttons for the eyes, then it's time to have a cuddle!

Variation

The legs can also be knitted in straight rows instead of in the round; in which case, change the yarn shade every second row rather than every row. As elsewhere, sew the sides together with mattress stitch.

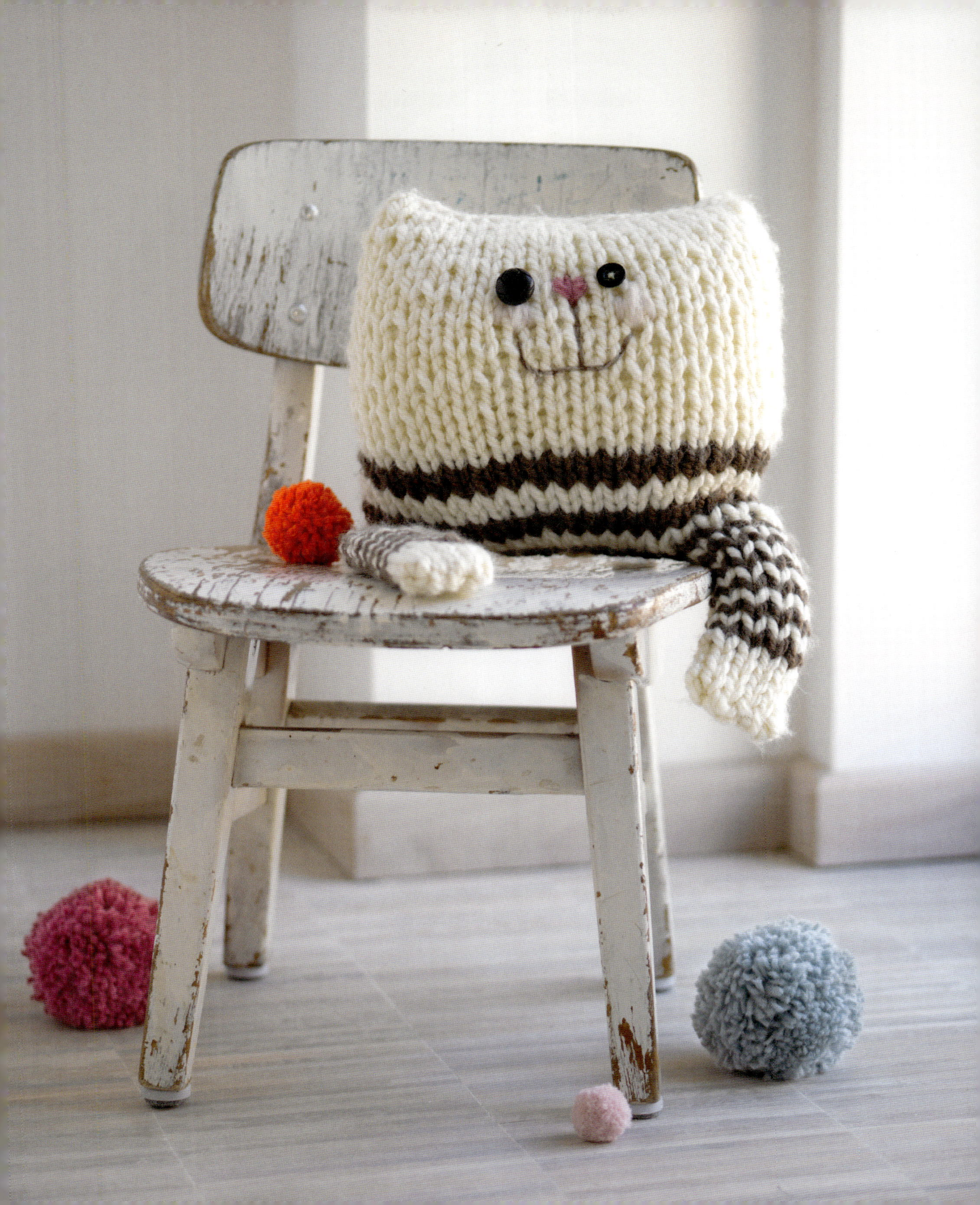

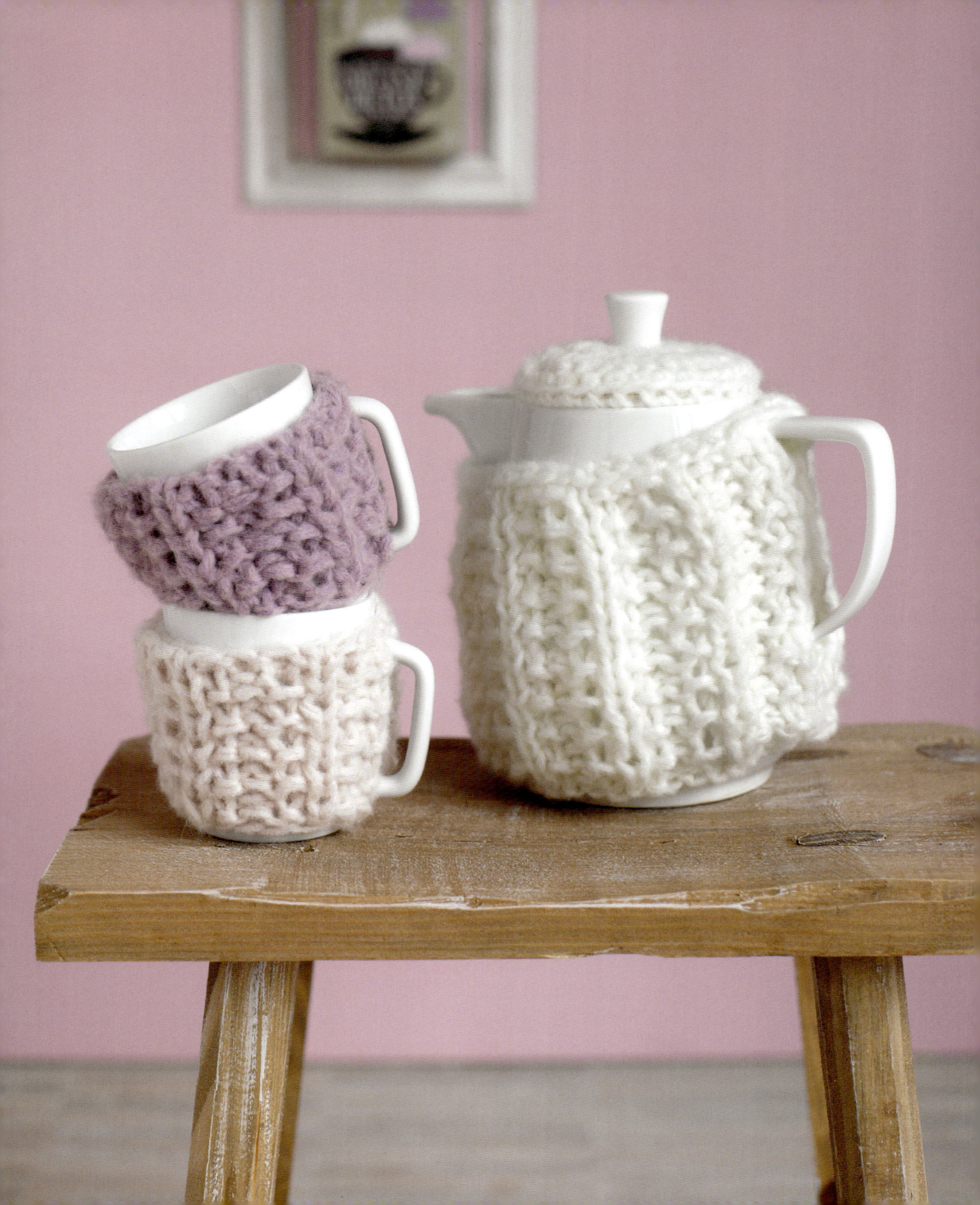

Mug and tea cosies

TIME 20 minutes per mug, 45 minutes for teapot

Moderate

SIZE Approx. 12 stitches to 10cm (4in), as the knitted fabric is very stretchy

Materials

Yarn

Schachenmayr select Apiretto, in 08119 (powder), 08125 (white), and 08105 (lilac)
Work with two strands of yarn.
Number of balls depends on the size of the item to be covered; usually one ball is enough

Other items

1 pair of 9mm (UK00/US13) needles
6mm hook

Instructions

The cosies are knitted; the teapot lid is crocheted.

To make the cosies, cast on stitches in a multiple of 4 to fit around the item, adding an extra 3 sts (see "Size" information above). Work up in rows in this basic pattern:
Row 1: [K3, p1] rep to last 3 sts, k3.
Row 2: [K1, p1, k2] rep to last 3 sts, k1, p1, k1.
Repeat these two rows until the work is the desired size. Cast off. Place the work around the mug or teapot and join the edges at the top and bottom with overcasting (see p.89), ensuring you leave a space for the handles.

To make the lid, work a foundation chain big enough to fit over the knob. Work in rounds in double crochet. Increase in every stitch in the first round, then in every second stitch in the following round until you have almost the right size. Finish with two rounds without increases.

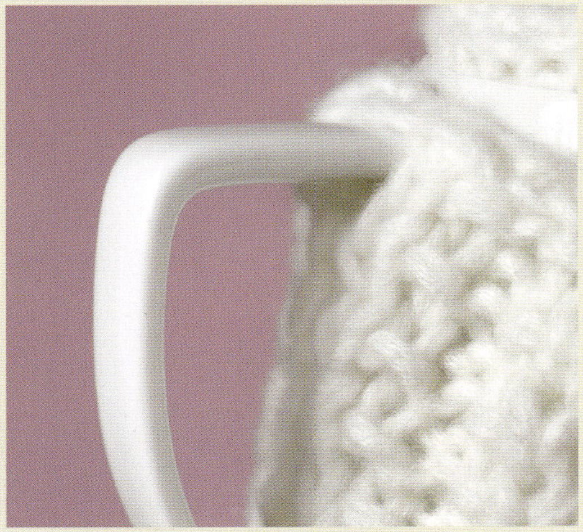

A space is left for the handle so that the knitted cover can be removed to enable the mug or teapot to be washed.

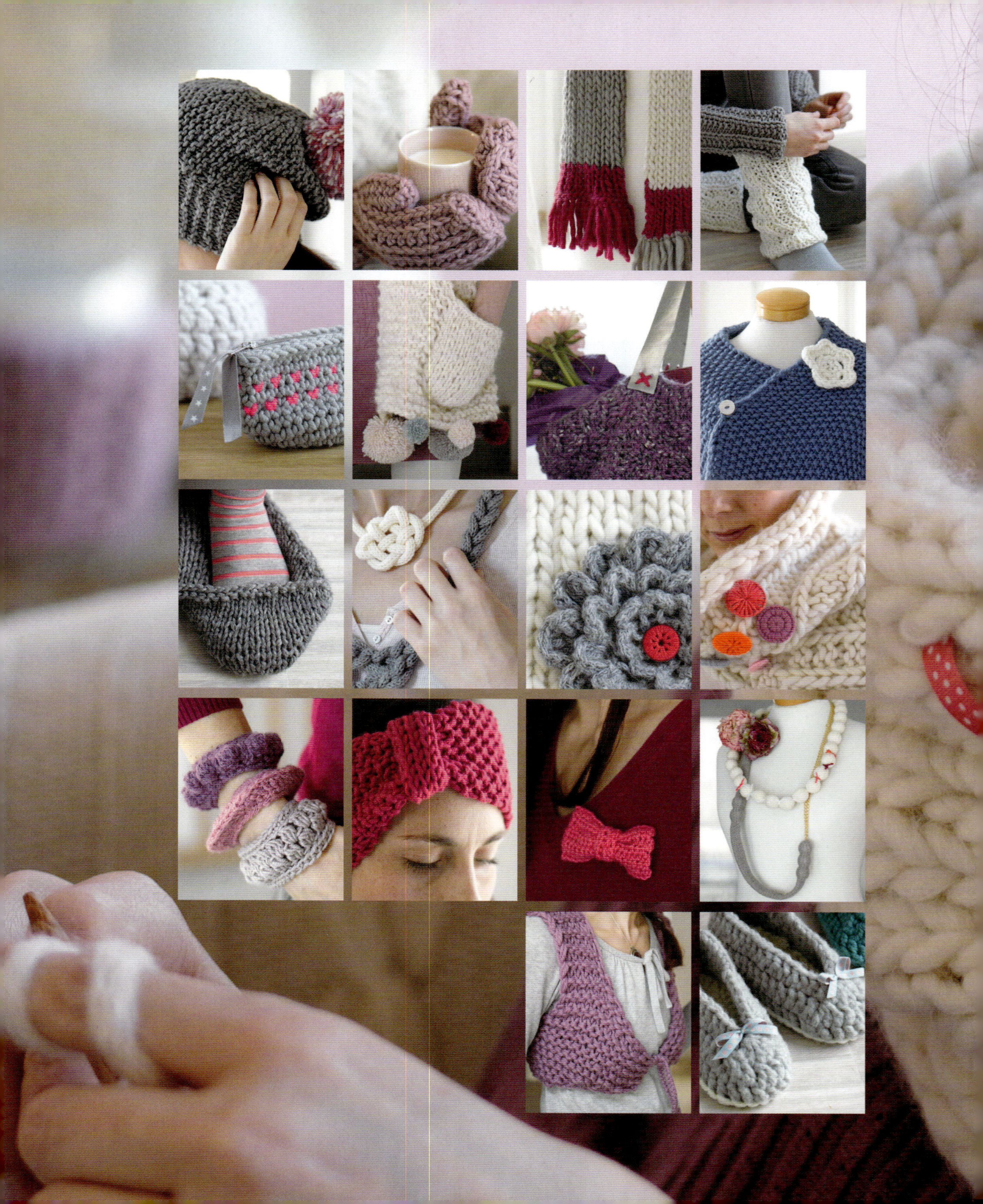

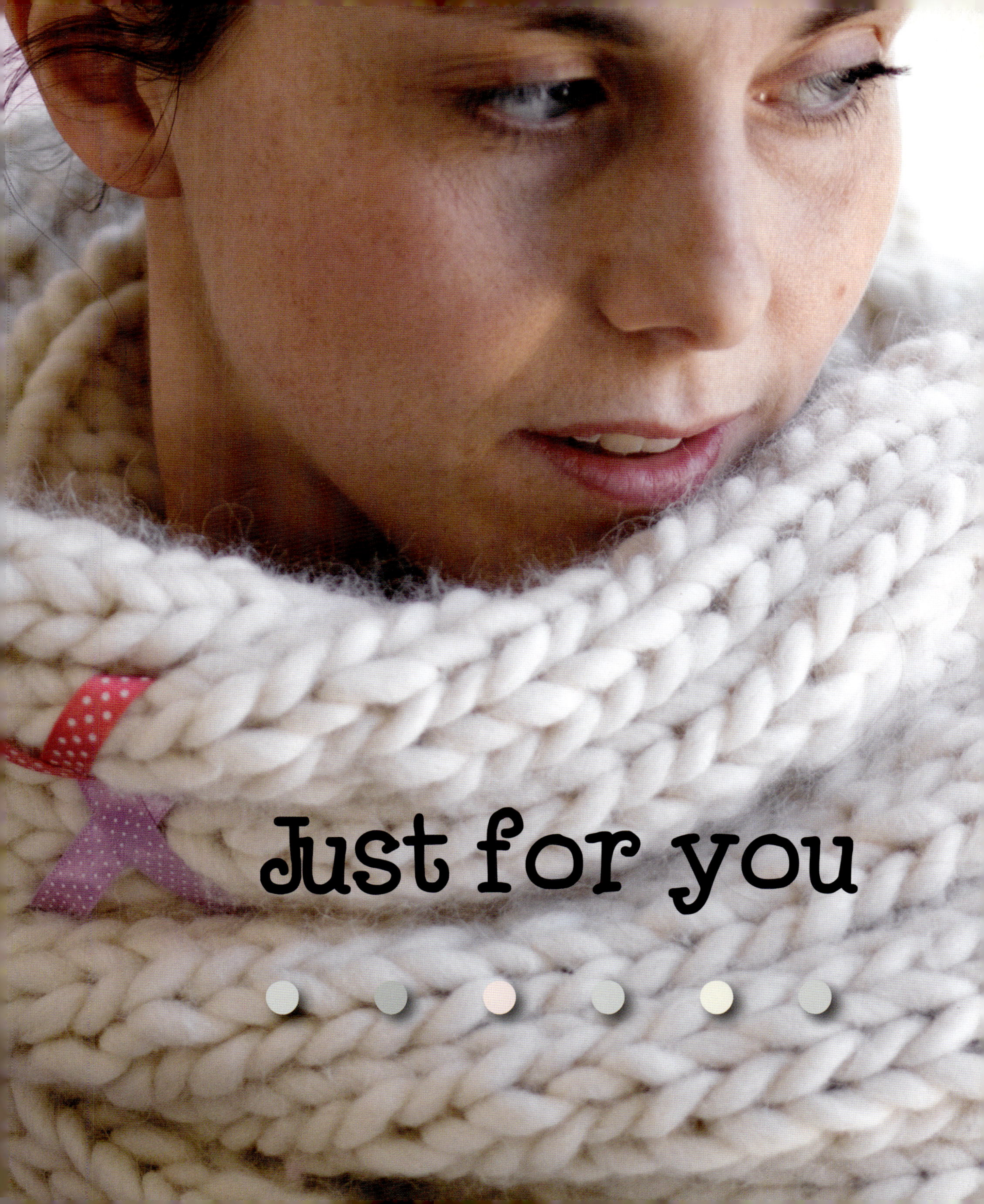

Just for you

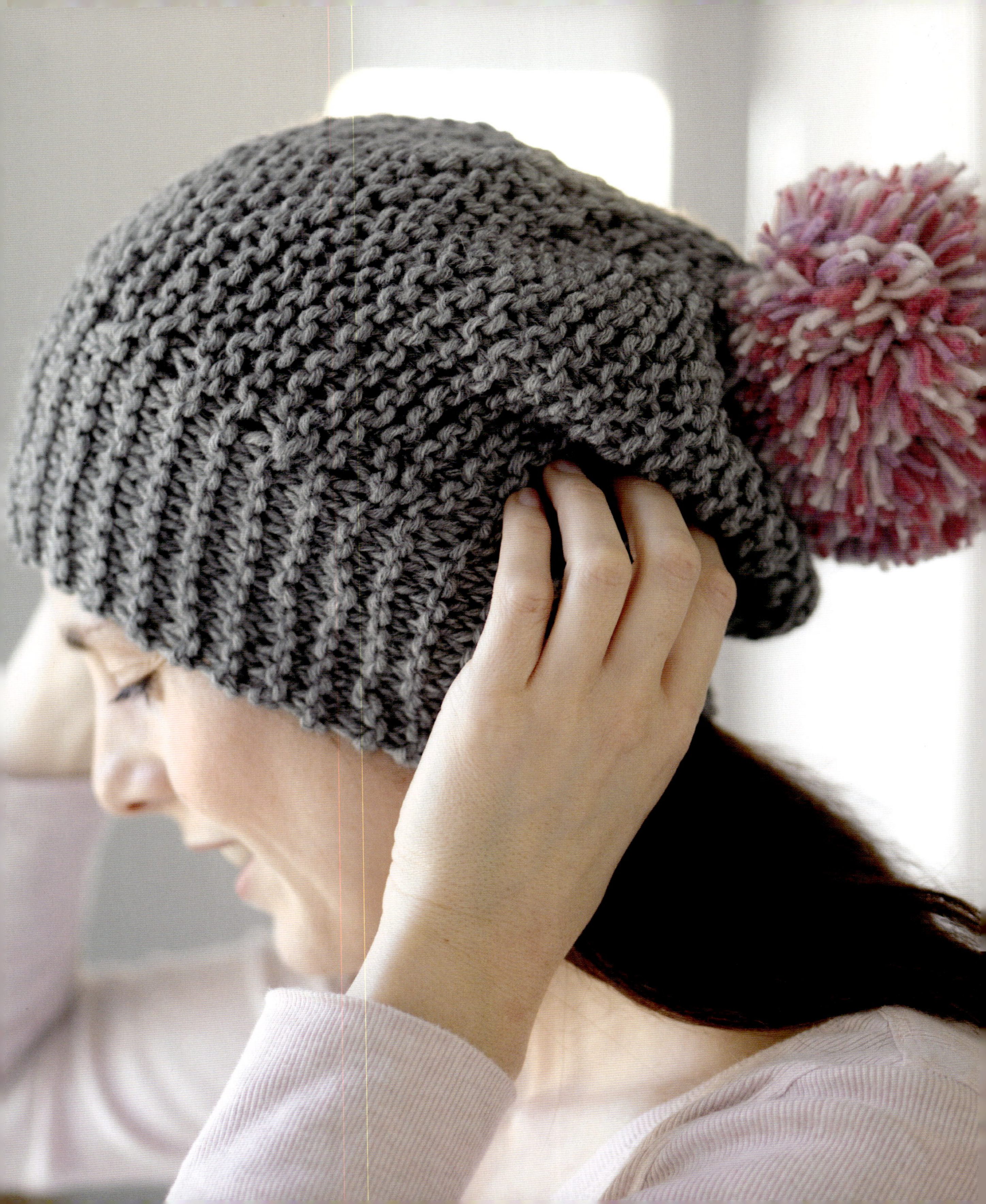

Bobble hat

TIME 2½ hours

Easy

SIZE Adaptable

Materials

Yarn for the hat

Schachenmayr original Boston, 100g in 00092 (mid grey)

Yarn for the pom-pom

Small amounts of Schachenmayr original Apiretto, in 08119 (powder), 08145 (raspberry), and 08105 (lilac)

Other items

1 pair of 7mm (UK2/US10½) needles

Instructions

This hat is knitted in rows in garter stitch. The rounded shape is achieved by knitting shortened rows (as for the baskets on page 12).
Cast on 30 stitches.

Row 1: K24, leave 6 rem sts on needle, turn.
Row 2: K14, leave rem sts on needle, turn.
Row 3: K.
Row 4: K.
Row 5: K26, leave 4 rem stitches on needle, turn.
Row 6: K.

Rep rows 1–6 as required.
Cast off when the hat is the desired size to fit your head. Graft the first and last rows together (see p.89). At the top of the hat, run a strand of yarn through the edge and draw it together. Finally, sew on the pink pom-pom.

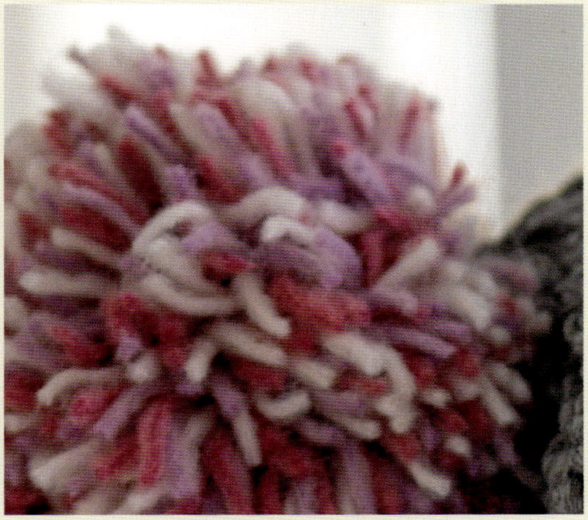

Instructions for making pom-poms are given on page 61. For the pom-pom shown here, you will need two rings of cardboard with an outer diameter of 12cm (5in) and an inner diameter of 5cm (2¼in).

Cosy mittens

TIME 2 hours

Moderate

SIZE Length 29cm (11½in)

Materials

Yarn

Rowan Big Wool, 200g in 00064 (Prize)

Other items

9mm hook

Instructions

Work 27 ch.

Row 1: Insert hook into third chain from hook, work htr to end, 2 ch, turn.

Row 2: Work in htr, but instead of inserting hook into the top two loops, insert it into the horizontal bar directly underneath; 3 htr in last st, 2 ch, turn.

Row 3: Work in htr, inserting hook into back loop only, 2 ch, turn.

Row 4: Work in htr, as for row 2, 2 ch, turn.

Row 5: Htr3tog, then htr as for row 3, 2 ch, turn.

Row 6: Work in htr, as for row 2, 2 ch, turn. This completes the back of the mitten. Now, continue with the front.

Row 7: Work htr in back loop of next 9 sts, 1 ss in back loop of next st, 9 ch, 1 htr in third ch from hook, 6 htr along chain; join with 1 ss on next-but-one stitch of glove; continue working htr in back loop to end, 2 ch, turn.

Row 8: Work in htr, as for row 2, along the thumb as well: work to tip of thumb in the same way as the rest of the row, then back along other side; miss bottom thumb stitch and first ch of palm, continue in htr to fingertips; 3 htr in last st, 2 ch, turn.

Row 9: Work in htr, as for row 3 to start of thumb, 1 ch, 5 ss along thumb, miss the two sts at thumb tip, 4 ss back down thumb, 14 htr to end of row; 2 ch, turn.

Row 10: Work in htr, as for row 2; when the bottom of the thumb is reached, continue from the other side of the thumb to the end; thumb section is now complete; 2 ch, turn.

Row 11: Htr3tog, htr as in row 3, 2 ch, turn.

Row 12: Work in htr, as for row 2. Fasten off. Sew up the mitten with overcasting (see p.89), including the thumb seam.

The left mitten is worked as a mirror image.

Work 27 ch.

Row 1: As for first mitten.

Row 2: 3 htr in first st, continue with htr, inserting hook into the horizontal bar underneath instead of the two top loops; 2 ch, turn.

Rows 3–4: Work as for first mitten.

Row 5: Work in htr, as for row 3 to last 3 sts, htr3tog, 2 ch, turn.
Row 6: Work as for first mitten.
Row 7: Work htr in back loop of next 11 sts, 1 ss in back loop of next st, 9 ch, 1 htr in third ch from hook, 6 htr along foundation ch, 1 ss on next-but-one st of glove to join; cont to work htr into back loop to end of row, 2 ch, turn.
Row 8: Work 3 htr in first stitch, then htr as in row 2 as far as thumb; miss last stitch of main glove and bottom thumb stitch, work to tip of thumb as for the rest of the row and down the other side again; work htr, 2 ch, turn.
Row 9: 13 htr as for row 3, 4 ss along thumb, miss two sts at tip of thumb, 5 ss back down thumb, 1 ch, cont to work htr, 2 ch, turn.
Row 10: Work as for first mitten.
Row 11: Work in htr, as for row 3 to last 3 sts, htr3tog, 2 ch, turn.
Row 12: Work as for first mitten.
Sew up.

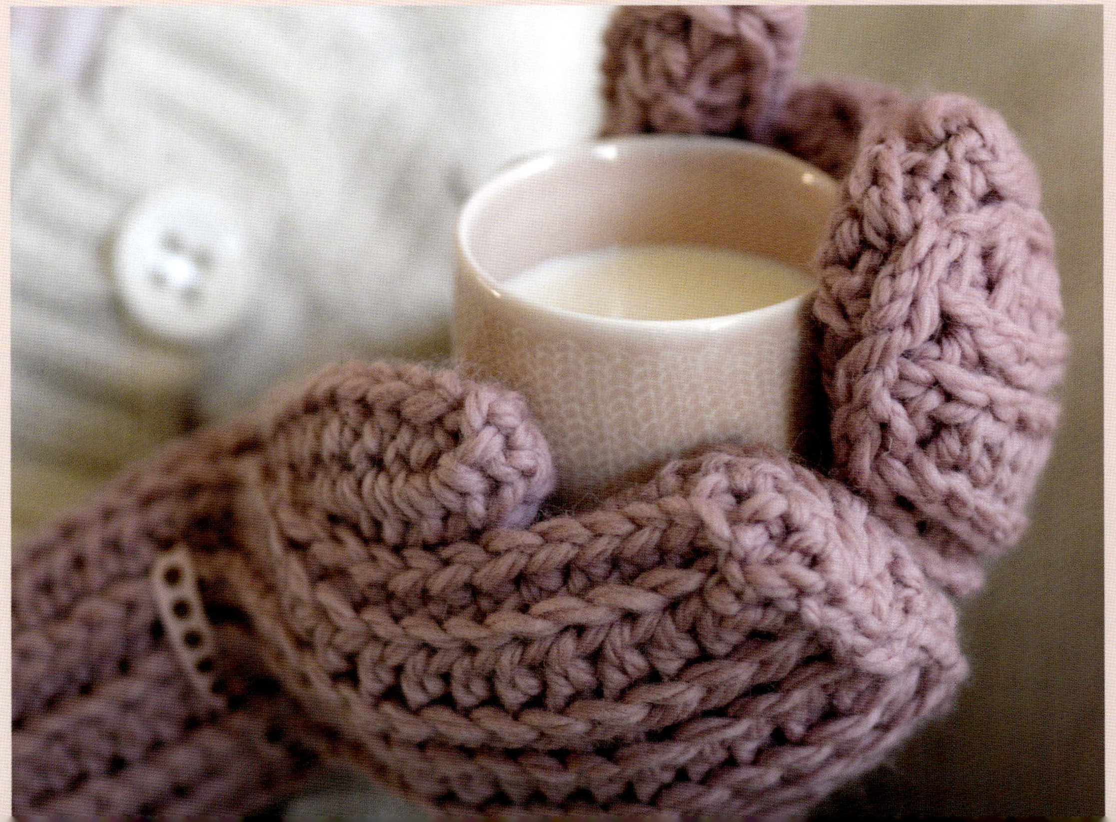

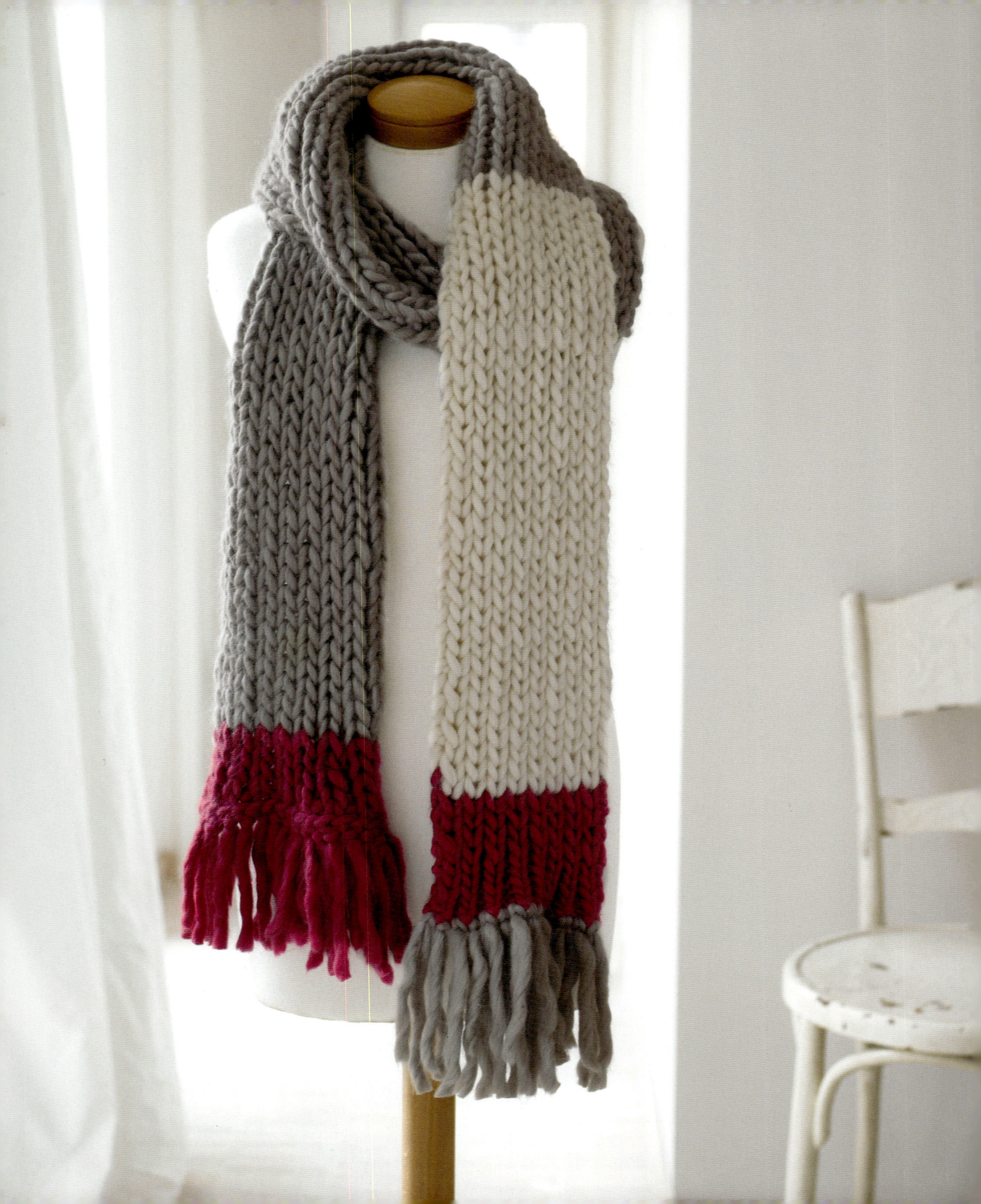

Tasselled scarf

Materials

Yarn

Schachenmayr select Highland Alpaca, 500g in 2979 (stone), 100g in 2945 (pink), and 100g in 2925 (cream)

Other items

1 pair of 12mm (US17) needles
Crochet hook for tassels

TIME 3 hours

Easy

SIZE Length 2.2m (87in) (without tassels), width 15cm (6in)

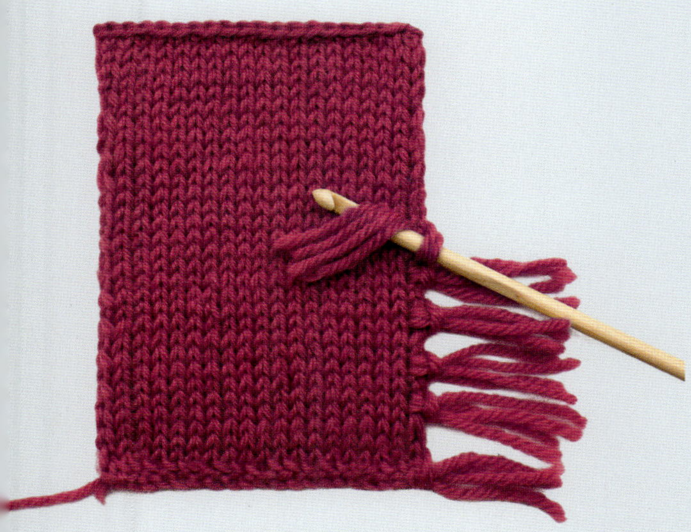

This lovely long scarf is the perfect project for those with little or no experience of knitting. All you have to do is knit and purl.

Instructions

Cast on 16 stitches in pink yarn. The pattern for this scarf is a simple rib:
Row 1: K1, p1.

Knit 5 rows in rib. Change to grey yarn and knit all 5 balls in rib, leaving some for the tassels. Change to white yarn and knit the whole ball in rib. Change back to pink, knit 10 rows in rib, and cast off.

Now for the decorative tassels. Cut a strip of cardboard that is slightly broader than the tassel length. Wind the yarn around the cardboard repeatedly, then cut through it on one side. This gives you a supply of yarn strands the same length. Fold two strands in half. Insert a crochet hook through the edge of the work from the back, pick up the middle of the strands and draw them a little way through. Pull the four yarn ends through the loop (see photo insert). Repeat until the row of tassels is complete.

Arm- and legwarmers

Materials

Yarn

Schachenmayr original Merino Super Big Mix, 100g per pair of armwarmers in 00192 (mid grey), 200g per pair of legwarmers in 00102 (white)

Other items

1 pair of 7mm (UK2/US10½) needles

TIME 1–1½ hours per warmer

Easy

SIZE Armwarmers, length 25cm (9¾in); leg warmers, length 45cm (17¾in)

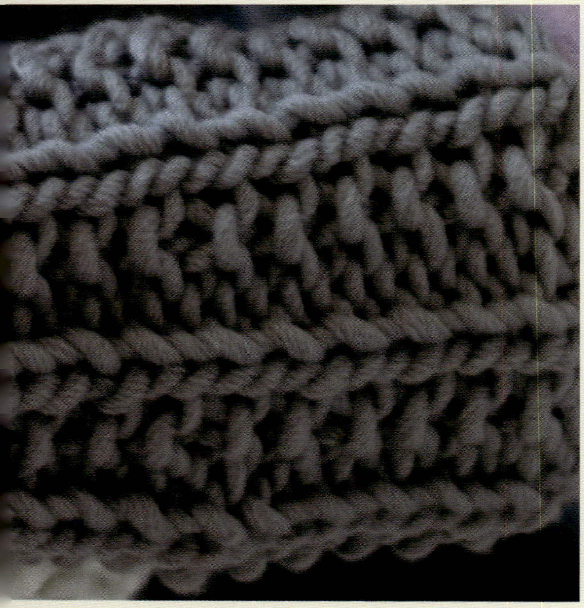

By alternating knit and purl stitches over two rows you get this thick, wonderfully stretchy pattern known as "mock fisherman's rib".

Instructions

For the legwarmers, cast on stitches in a multiple of 4. In our version there are 20 stitches for the armwarmers and 28 for the legwarmers. Work in rows in the following pattern:
Row 1: K3, p1, rep to end.
Row 2: K2, *p1, k3 to last 2 sts, p1, k1.
Keep repeating these rows.

Cast off when the desired length has been reached (in our version, after 35 rows for the armwarmers, and 60 rows for the legwarmers). Sew the side seams together with mattress stitch (see p.89).

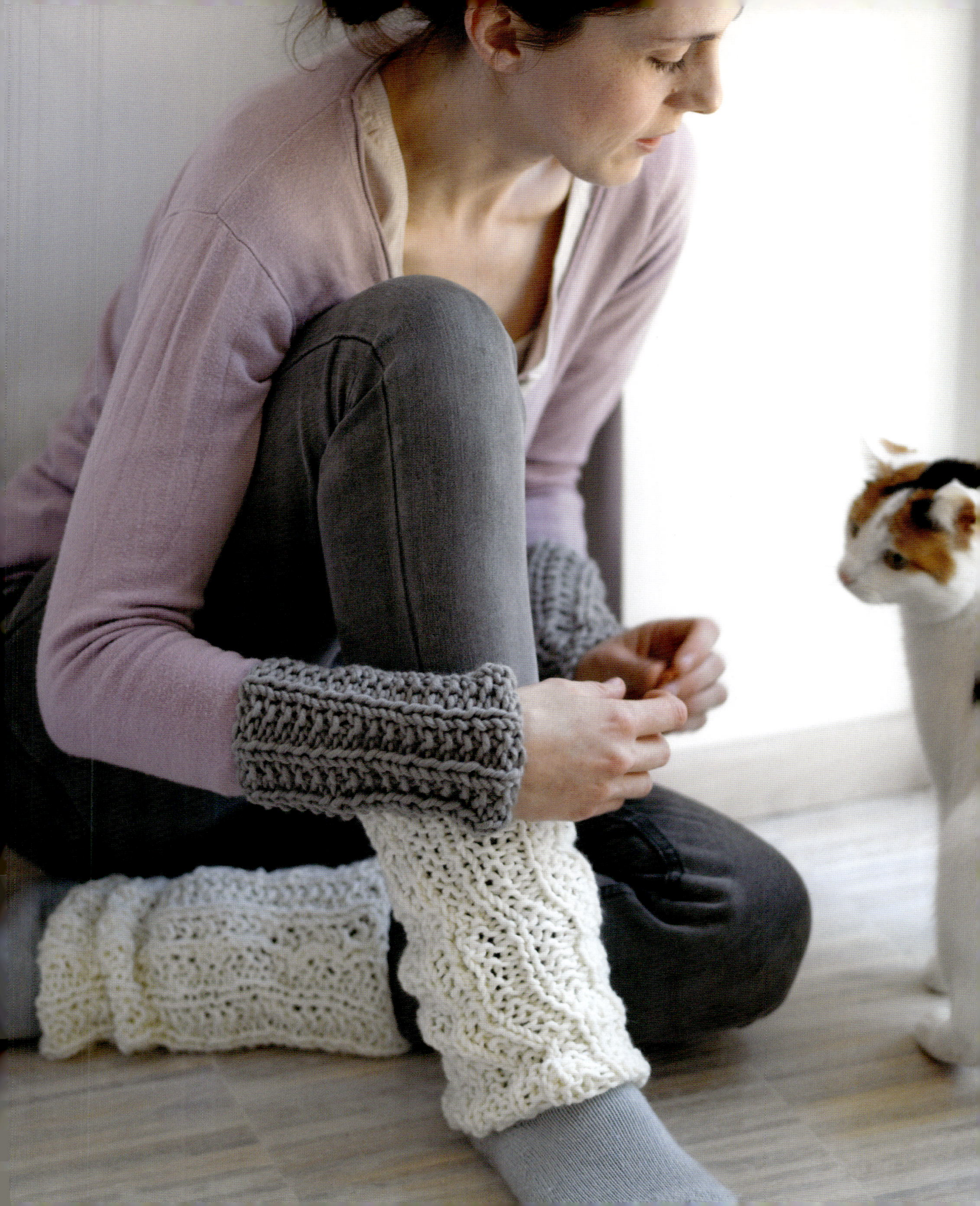

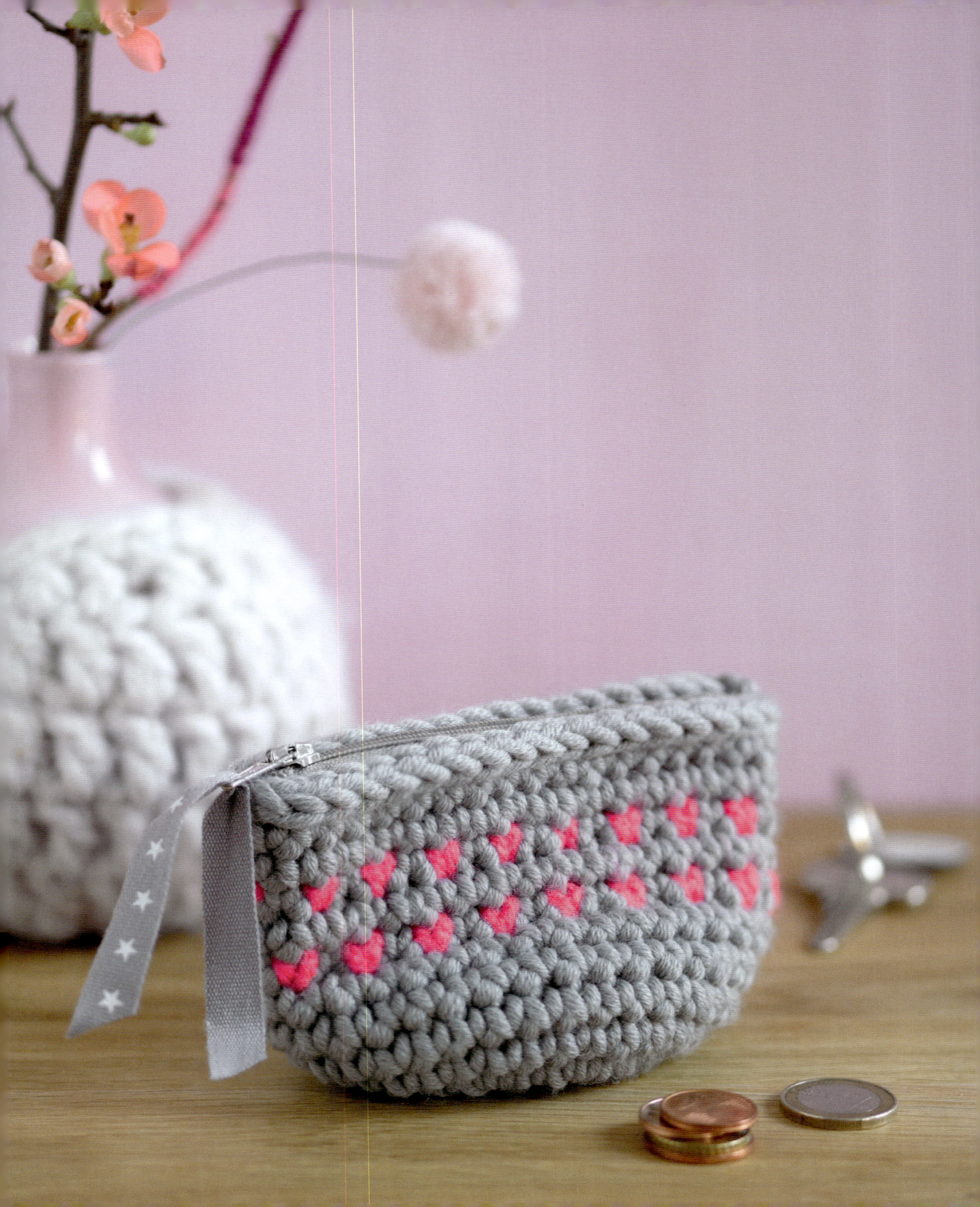

Zippy purse

TIME 45 minutes

Easy

SIZE Height 7cm (2¾in), width 13cm (5in)

Materials

Yarn

Schachenmayr original Merino Super Big Mix, 100g in 00090 (grey)

Schachenmayr original Bravo Big, yarn oddments in 00136 (pink)

Other items

5mm hook

10cm (4in) zip

Matching sewing thread

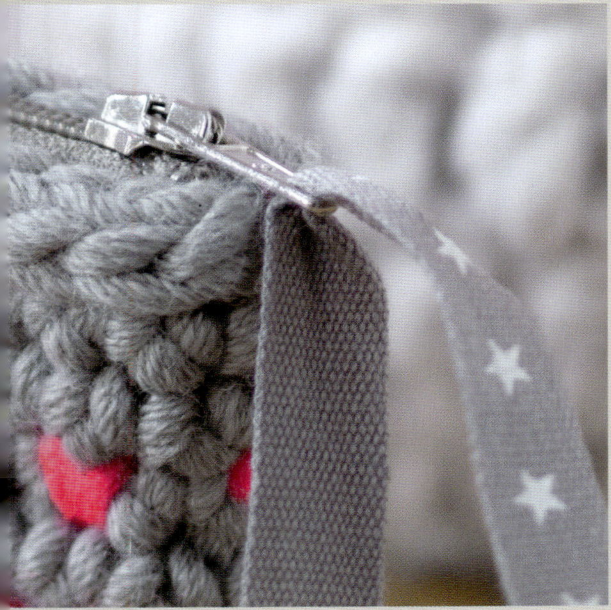

You can also thread a pretty silk ribbon through the zip's pull tab.

Instructions

In a foundation ring (see p.95) work 6 dc. Mark the first st of each round with a small safety pin. Work in grey in rounds as follows:

Round 1: 2 dc in each st (12 sts).
Round 2: 2 dc in each st (24 sts).
Round 3: 1 and 2 dc alternately (36 sts).
Rounds 4–7: Dc (12 sts).
Round 8: Work the coloured dots dc as well; work first st in pink yarn, changing to grey yarn on step 3 of instructions (see p.91), and work foll dc with grey; repeat, swapping colours for each st.
Round 9: Dc in grey.
Round 10: As for round 8, but start with first dc in grey; cont to alternate pink and grey.
Rounds 11–12: Dc in grey. Fasten off, and sew zip into opening using matching thread.

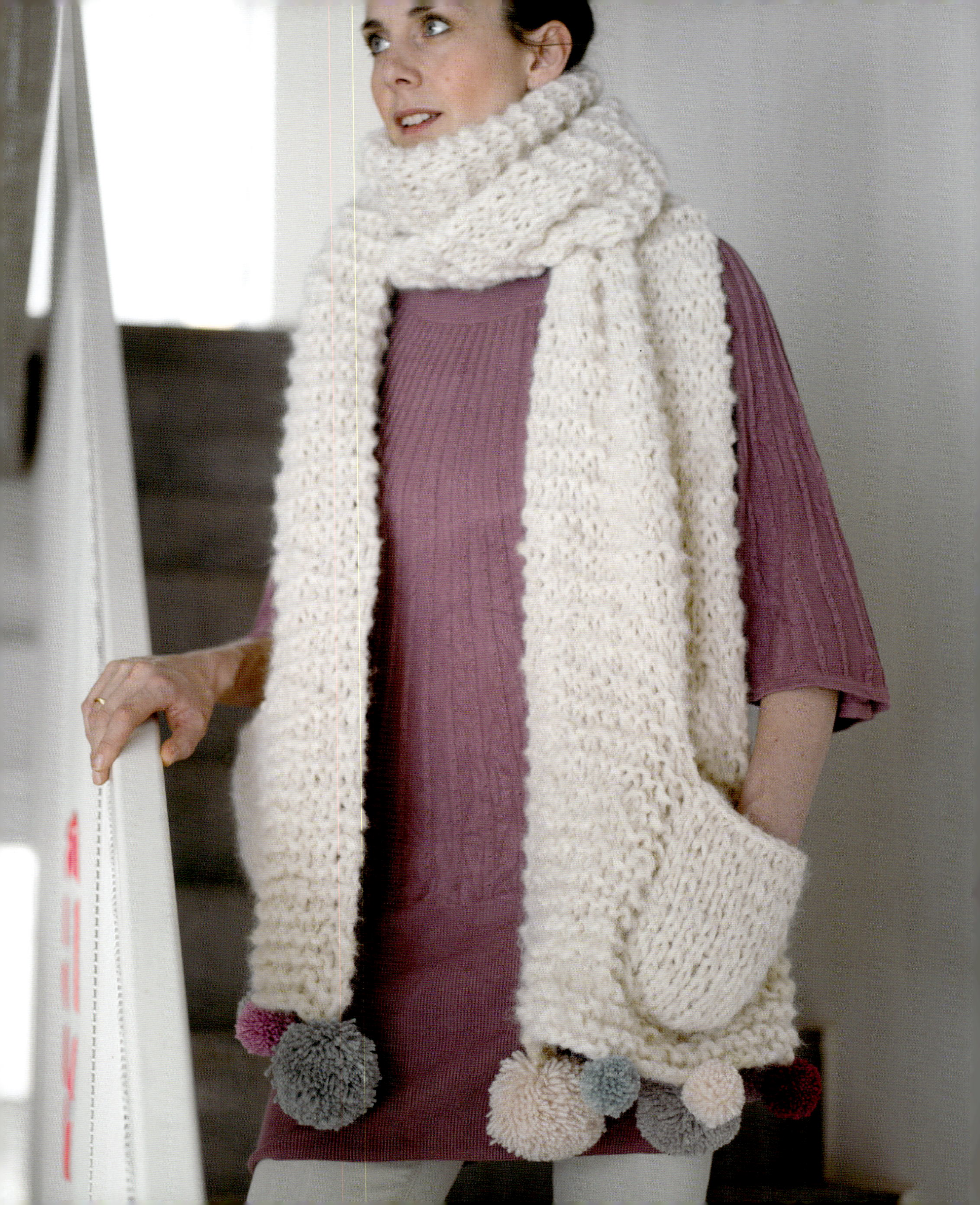

Pom-pom scarf with pockets

TIME 4 hours

Easy

SIZE 2m × 50cm
(79 x 20in)

Materials

Yarn

Schachenmayr select Alegretto, 350g in 08525 (natural)
Yarn oddments for pom-poms

Other items

15mm (US19) circular needles
1 pair of 9mm (UK00/US13) needles

Instructions

Using the 15mm needles cast on 35 stitches. Knit in rows in garter stitch until the scarf measures approx. 2m (79in). Our version uses 6½ balls of yarn. Cast off.

For the pockets (make 2): with 9mm needles cast on 16 stitches and work 20 rows stocking stitch. Cast off. Cut the yarn, leaving a generous tail; use this to sew the pockets onto the scarf with mattress stitch (see p.89).

Make pom-poms of different sizes and sew them onto the scarf ends.

How to make pom-poms

Draw two circles (diameter 12cm/5in) on a piece of cardboard, then another circle (diameter 5cm/2¼in) inside each with the same centre. Cut out the cardboard rings. Cut a few strands of yarn approx. 100cm (39in) long and wind them in a ball. Place the rings together, matching them exactly. Wind the yarn tightly and evenly around the cardboard rings. If necessary, cut more strands and keep winding.
When the hole in the centre becomes too narrow, thread more yarn into a blunt-ended needle and continue to wind it round the ring. Once the hole is completely filled, insert one point of a pair of scissors between the outer edges of the cardboard rings and cut through all the strands. Insert a double strand of yarn between the rings, pull tightly, and knot the ends together. Remove the cardboard rings. Fluff out the pom-pom and trim into shape if it's uneven. Do not cut off the middle strands, as you will need them to fasten the pom-poms in place. By increasing or decreasing the size of the cardboard rings you will be able to make larger or smaller pom-poms.

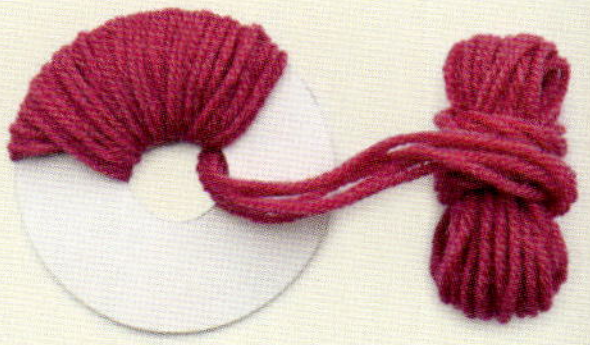

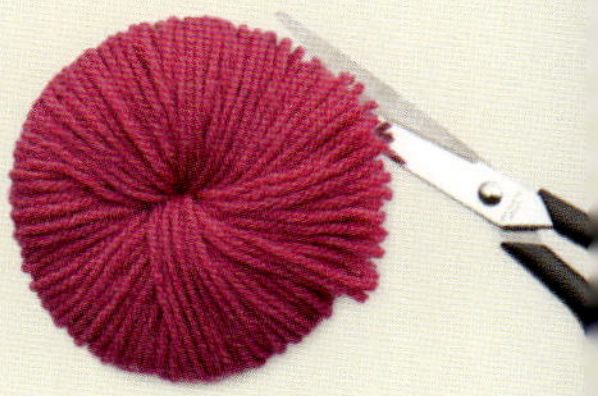

There are also handy pom-pom makers available commercially (for example, by Clover or Prym) – an easy way to make various sizes of pom-pom.

Tweedy tote bag

TIME 3 hours

Easy

SIZE Height 40cm (16in), width 35cm (14in)

Materials

Yarn

Schachenmayr select Tweed Deluxe, 200g in 07105 (lilac/grey) and 100g in 07114 (black/white)

Work with two strands of yarn.

Other items

6mm (UK4/US10) circular needle, 60cm (23½in) long

2 leather straps, approx. 20cm (8in) long

Hole punch

4 small pieces of leather (approx. 3 x 3cm/ 1¼ x 1¼in) for reinforcing on the reverse

Contrasting yarn

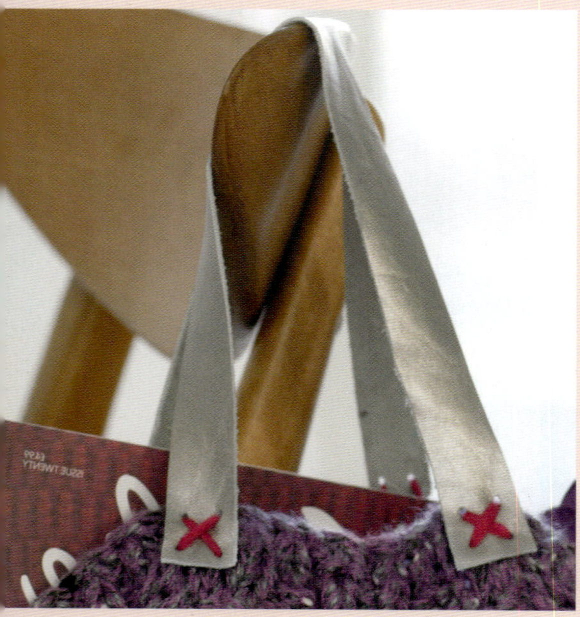

Instead of leather straps, you can also use ready-made bag handles from a haberdashery shop. They come in a wide range of materials and lengths.

Instructions

Cast on 96 stitches in lilac. Join to knit in the round. Work 3 rounds in k1, p1 rib.

Continue in the following pattern: [K3, p3] for 3 rounds; [p3, k3] for 3 rounds; rep until you have worked 27cm (10½in).

Change colour and knit another 9cm (3½in) in k1, p1 rib.

Divide the stitches onto two needles. Place the needles alongside each other and graft together with Kitchener stitch (see p.24).

Punch four holes in the ends of the leather straps and in the same position in the small leather pieces. Sew the straps on using contrasting yarn, at the same time sewing a small leather square on the inside of each strap end to strengthen it.

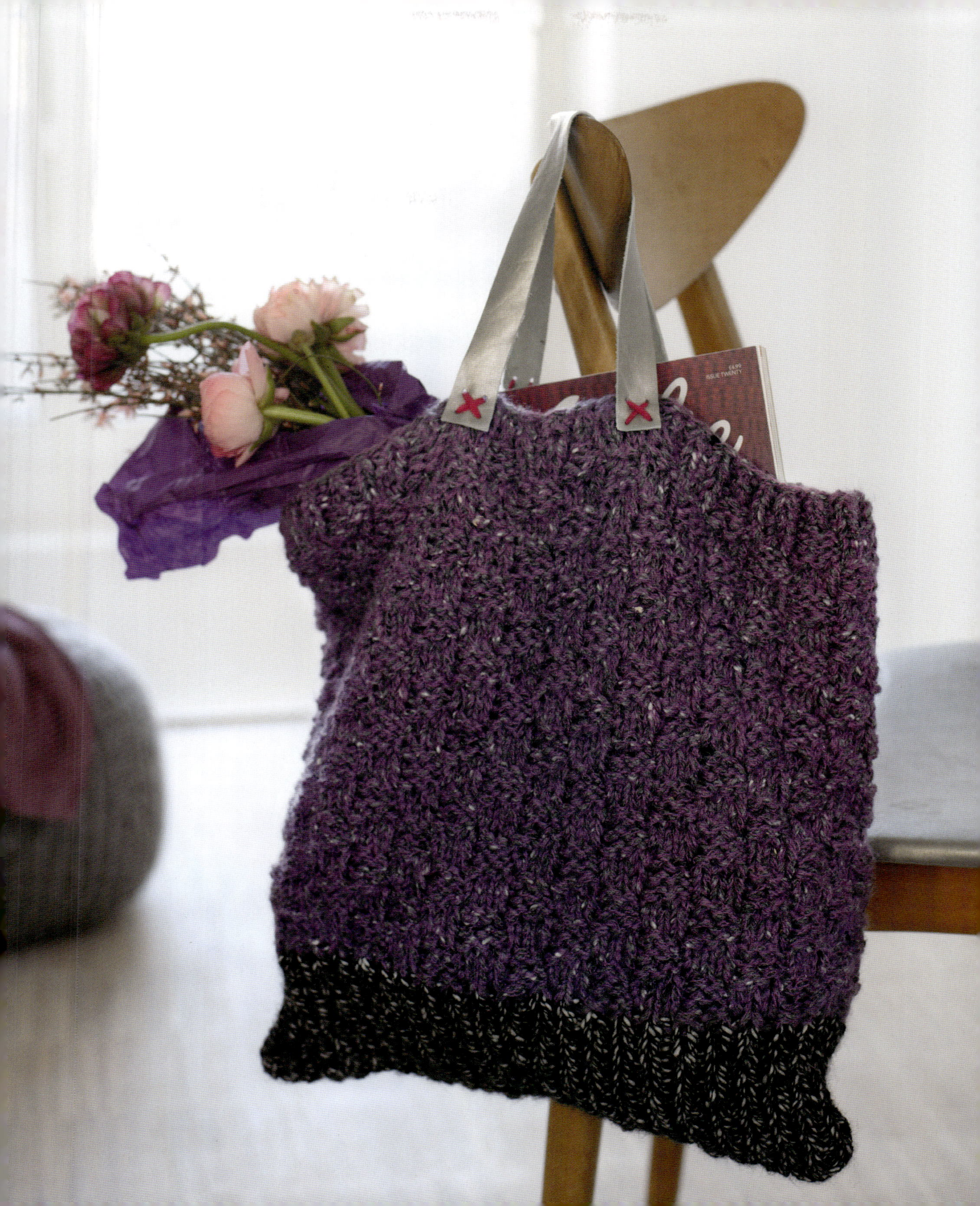

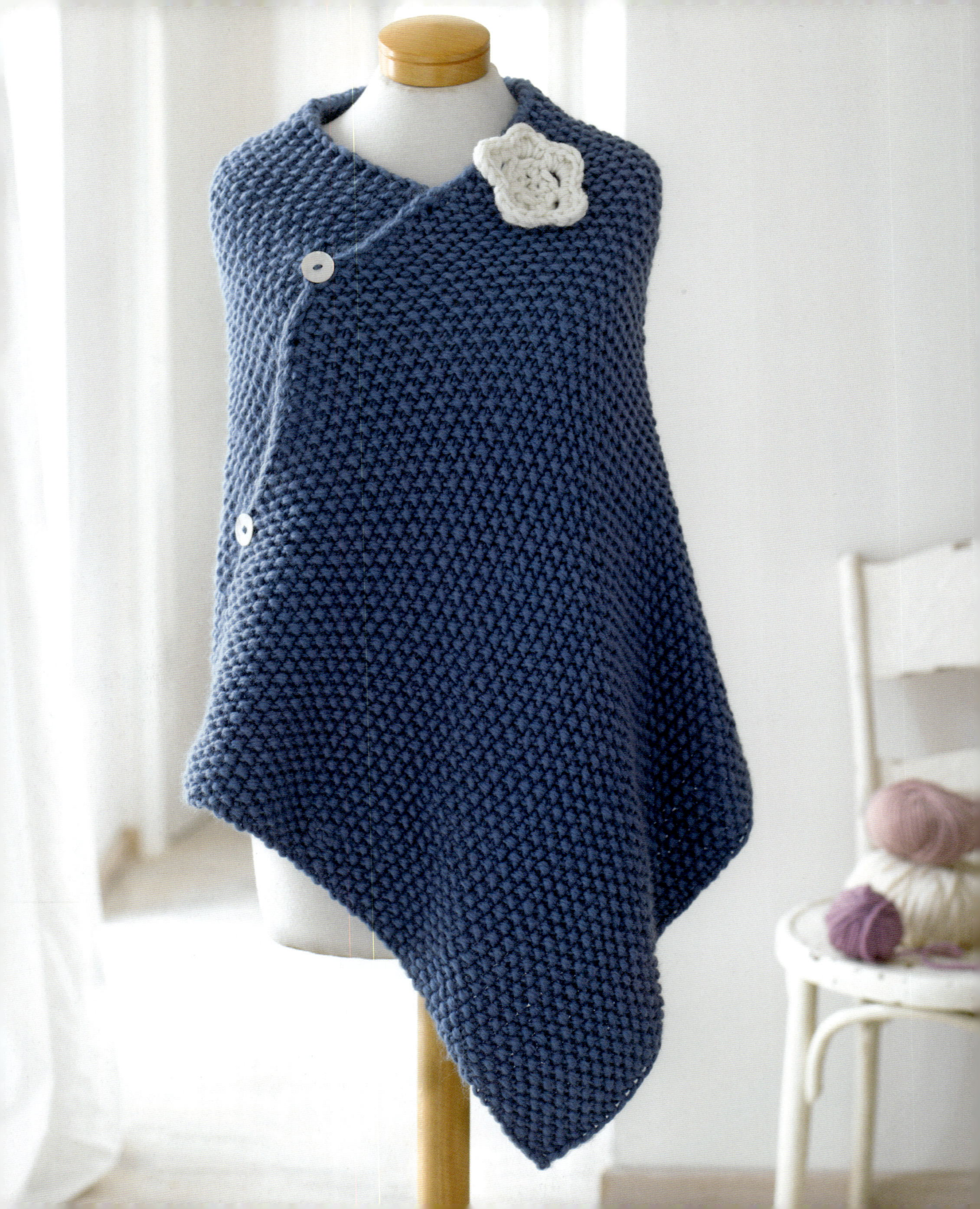

Poncho

TIME 10 hours

Easy

SIZE 58 × 1.3m (22¾ x 51in), clothing sizes UK 8–10 (36–38)

Materials

Yarn

Rowan Big Wool, 800g in 00052 (steel blue)

Other items

1 pair of 10mm (UK000/US15) needles

3 buttons

Instructions

Cast on 54 stitches.

Row 1: S1 knitwise; [k1, p1] rep to last st, k1.

Row 2: S1 knitwise; [p1, k1] rep to last st, k1.

Rep rows 1 and 2 until work measures 1.3m (51in). Cast off.

Place one side of the poncho onto the other side so that points A and B match (see diagram). Sew up from A to B with an invisible seam (see p.89 for mattress stitch). You can decorate the seam with three or more buttons and a crocheted brooch (see below for instructions) if desired.

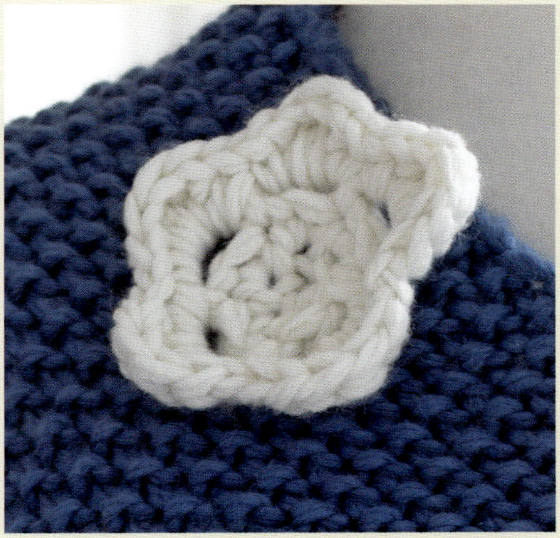

The brooch is worked with two strands of yarn using a 7mm hook and Schachenmayr original Merino Super Big Mix yarn. In a foundation ring (see p.95) work 5 dc and close with 1 ss.

Round 1: 2 dc in each st (10 sts), ending with 1 ss.

Round 2: (3 ch, miss next stitch of previous round, 1 ss in following stitch), rep to end.

Round 3: In 1st arc of chain, work 1 ss, 1 dc, 1 htr, 2 tr, 1 htr, 1 dc. Work round the following arcs in the same way. End round with 1 ss.

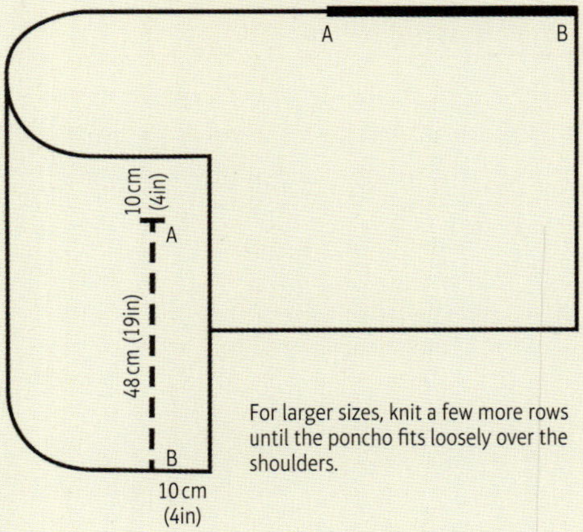

For larger sizes, knit a few more rows until the poncho fits loosely over the shoulders.

Cosy footwarmer

TIME 12½ hours

Moderate

SIZE 35 × 40cm (14 x 16in)

Materials

Yarn

Schachenmayr original Aventica, 150g in 00100 (storm mix)

Other items

1 pair of 9mm (UK00/US13) needles
Polyester soft toy stuffing

Instructions

Start at the tip of the heart. Cast on 2 stitches.

Row 1: P2.
Row 2: Knit into back and front of first st on left needle (that is, make 1 extra st); rep in 2nd stitch. (4 sts)
Row 3: P4.
Work in stocking stitch.

In every following knit row, increase in first and last sts as above. Purl alternate rows. Rep until you have 40 sts on the needle. Work 4 rows straight stocking stitch.
For right heart curve: k2tog, k16, k2tog, turn, p to end.
Foll rows: k2tog, k to last two sts, k2tog, turn, p to end. Rep these 2 rows until 8 sts remain. Cast off. Work left heart curve in same way.
Knit a second heart as above.

To make the foot pocket, cast on 40 stitches.
Rows 1–3: P.
Row 4: K.
Row 5: P.
Decrease as for the large heart shapes: k2tog, k16, k2tog, turn, p to end. Foll rows: k2tog, k to last 2 sts, k2tog, turn, p to end. Rep until 8 sts remain. Cast off. Work the left heart curve in the same way.
Place the two large pieces on top of each other, right sides out, and fit the small piece on top. Sew together with mattress stitch (see p.89), leaving a small opening. Stuff the heart with the stuffing material and close up to finish.

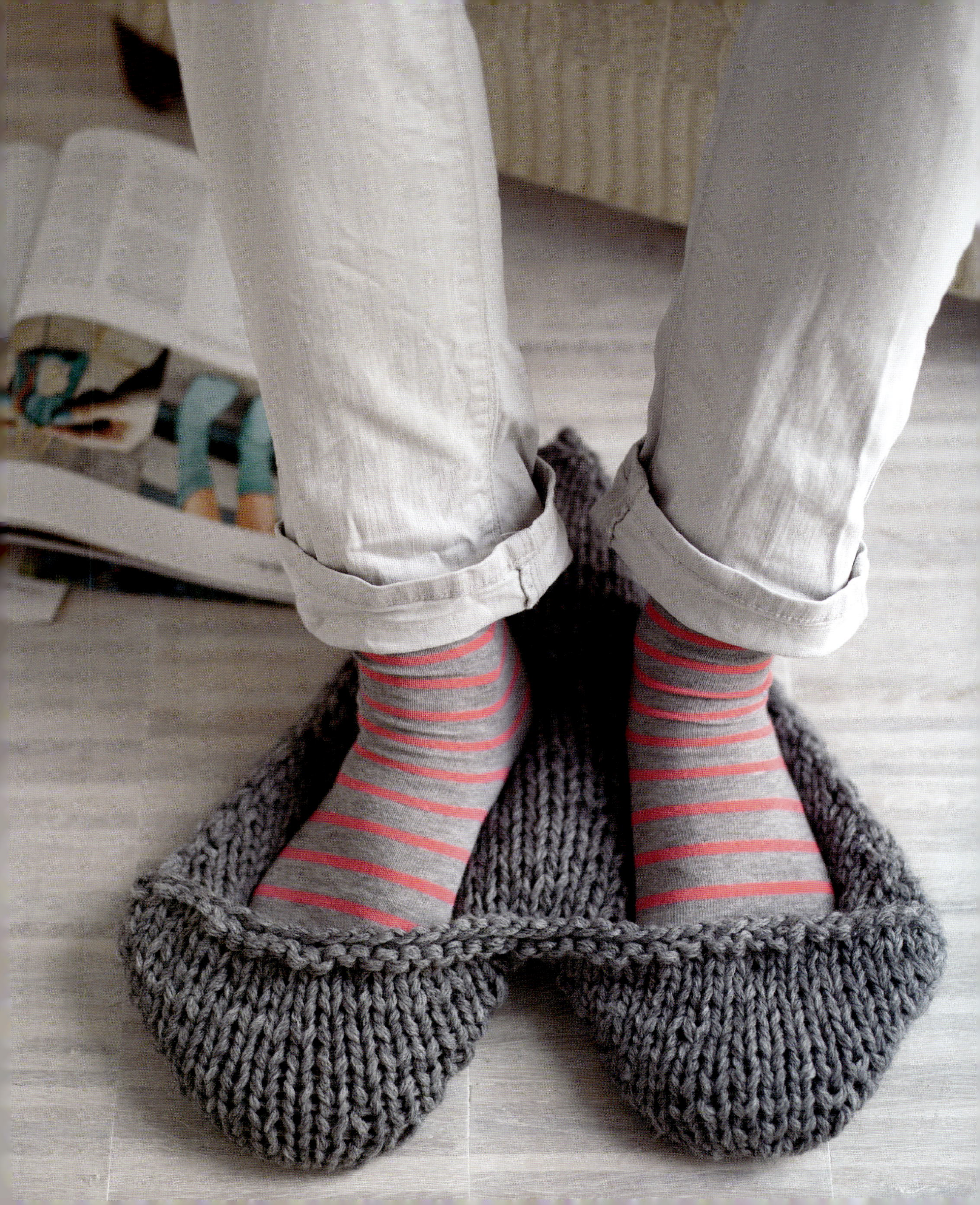

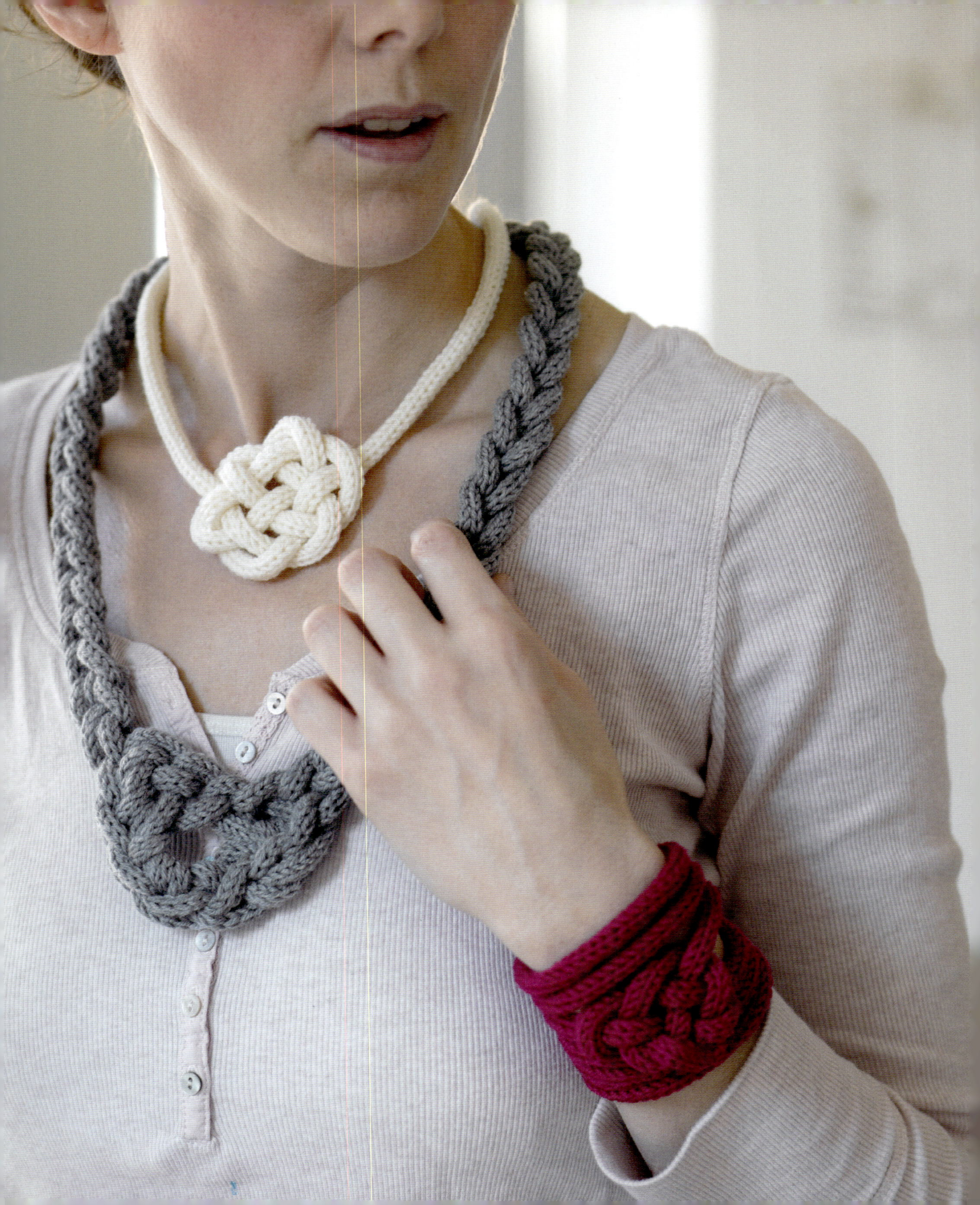

French-knitted jewellery

TIME 45 minutes per necklace/armband

Moderate

SIZE Your choice

Materials

Yarn

Schachenmayr original Extra Merino, 50g in 00092 (mid-grey mix), 00002 (cream), and 00037 (cyclamen)

Other items

Knitting mill or French knitter

20mm hook

Necklace clasps

Instructions

Make long tubes using the knitting mill or French knitter, or by hand. For each necklace with simple knots you need a tube length of approx. 1m (39in), and as much as 2m (79in) for the crocheted tube. It can be a lengthy process, but with a knitting mill you can do it in next to no time.

The long tubes are then knotted, woven, or crocheted, in whatever way your imagination takes you. You can also make great headbands, belts, or pendants from French-knitted tubes, as well as necklaces and armbands.

The white and pink tubes were knotted in a Celtic motif (see illustrations below). The tube ends can be joined simply by sewing them together or using clasps.

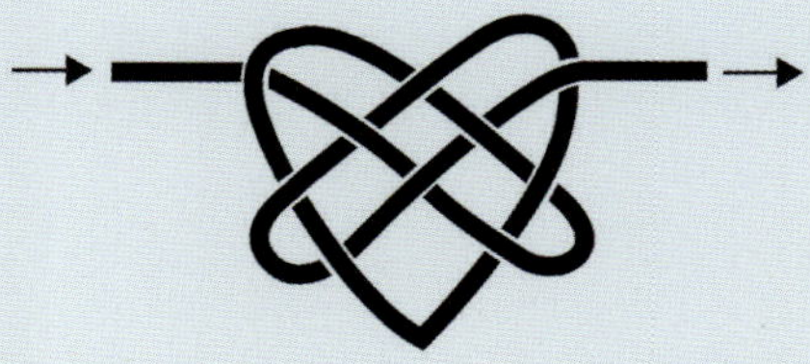

How to knot the white necklace

The grey necklace is crocheted. With a 20mm hook, work a foundation chain of 50 ch. Close the ring with 1 ss. Work 1 dc in next st, 3 dc in next st, 1 dc in next st and fasten with 1 ss in next st. Weave in the ends on the wrong side to conceal and sew up.

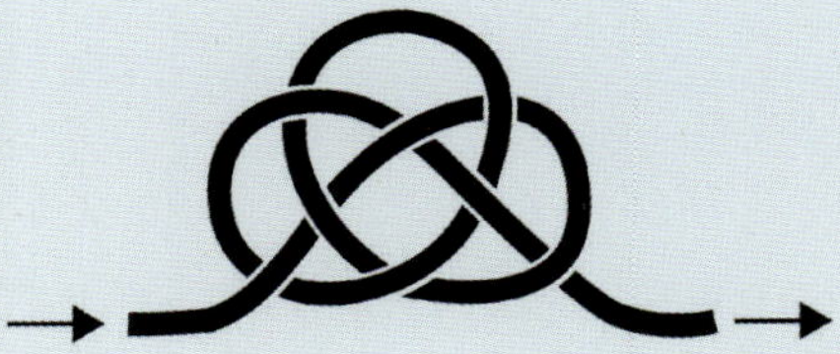

How to knot the armband

Flower brooch

TIME 30 minutes

Moderate

SIZE Diameter approx. 15cm (6in)

Materials

Yarn

Rowan Lima, 50g in 880 (Andes)

Other items

5mm hook

Brooch pin

Sewing needle and matching thread

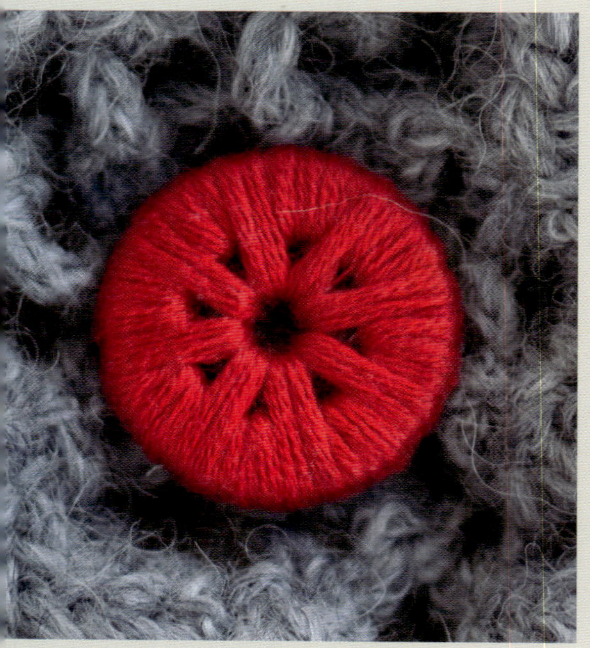

You can also decorate the centre of the brooch with a contrasting button. The one shown here is home-made. For this you will need Prym's "creative buttons" – transparent plastic buttons in two sizes that can be embroidered individually using wool or embroidery thread (available online or from haberdashery shops).

Instructions

Work 31 ch.

Row 1: 1 dc in second st from hook, (2 ch, 1 dc in next-but-one st); rep to end of chain, turn.

Row 2: 1 ss in first ch loop, 1 ch, 3 htr around first chain arc of previous row, 1 ch, 1 ss in same chain arc, 1 ss in next chain arc, 1 ch, 3 htr, 1 ch, 1 ss; work pattern 3 times: the basic principle is the same, but for next 3 arcs, work 4 htr, and foll 3 arcs with 4 tr; foll 3 arcs with 6 tr, next 3 arcs with 6 dtr, foll 3 with 8 dtr, and the rem with 8 trtr.

You end up with a long, undulating strip, which is then twisted round in a spiral to make a flower. The small petals sit on the inside and the large ones on the outside. The petals are held together with a few invisible stitches on the wrong side to hold the brooch in shape. Finish off by sewing the flower onto the brooch pin.

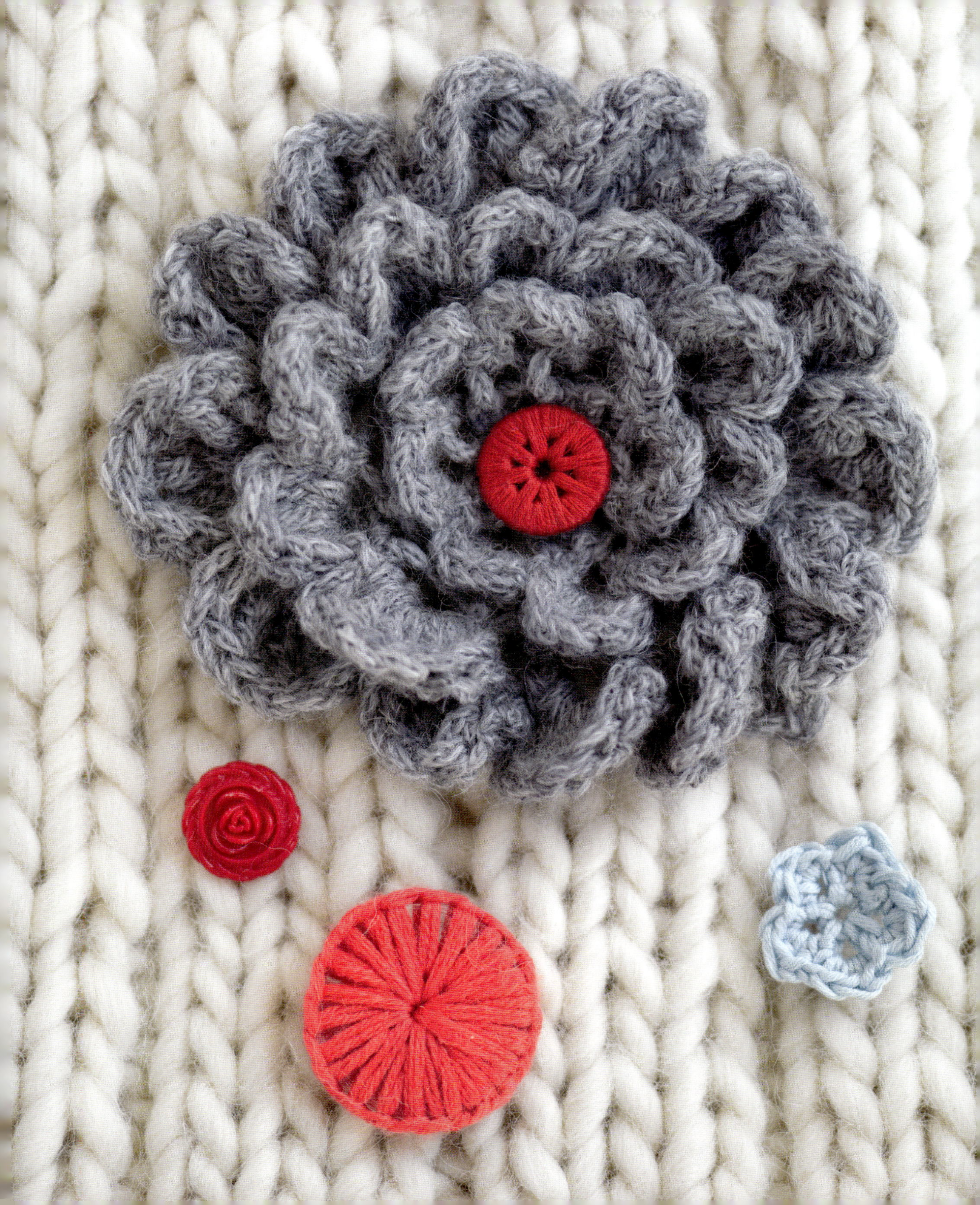

Loop scarf

TIME 2½ hours

Easy

SIZE Circumference 80cm (32in), width 35cm (14in)

Materials

Yarn

Schachenmayr select Highland Alpaca, 400g in 02925 (cream)

Other items

1 pair of 15mm (US19) needles

Decorative buttons (see p.70)

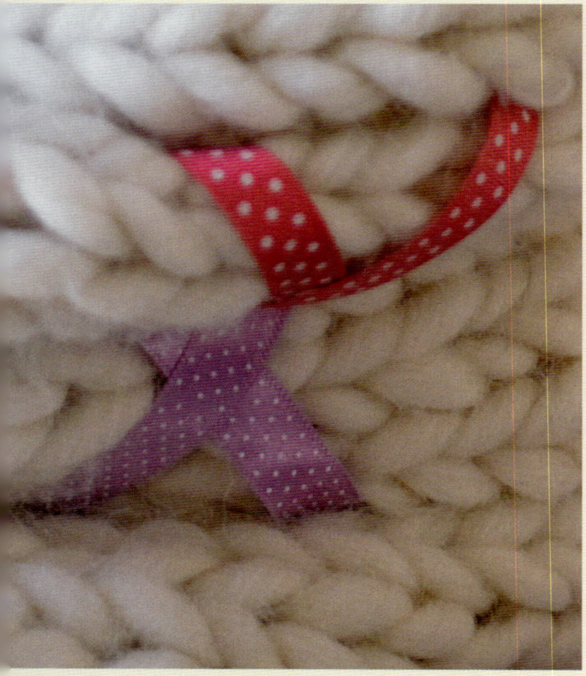

The scarf looks different when reversed, as if it has been worked in stocking stitch. In this photo the back is decorated with narrow, spotted silk ribbons.

Instructions

To make this loop scarf, cast on 32 stitches. Work in rows, following this basic pattern:

Row 1: [K3, p1] to end.

Row 2: [K1, p3] to end.

When the work measures 80cm (32in), cast off. Graft the start and end of the scarf into a loop (see p.89). Finish off by sewing on some decorative buttons.

Variations

For a wider or narrower scarf, cast on more or fewer stitches. Just make sure the number is a multiple of four.

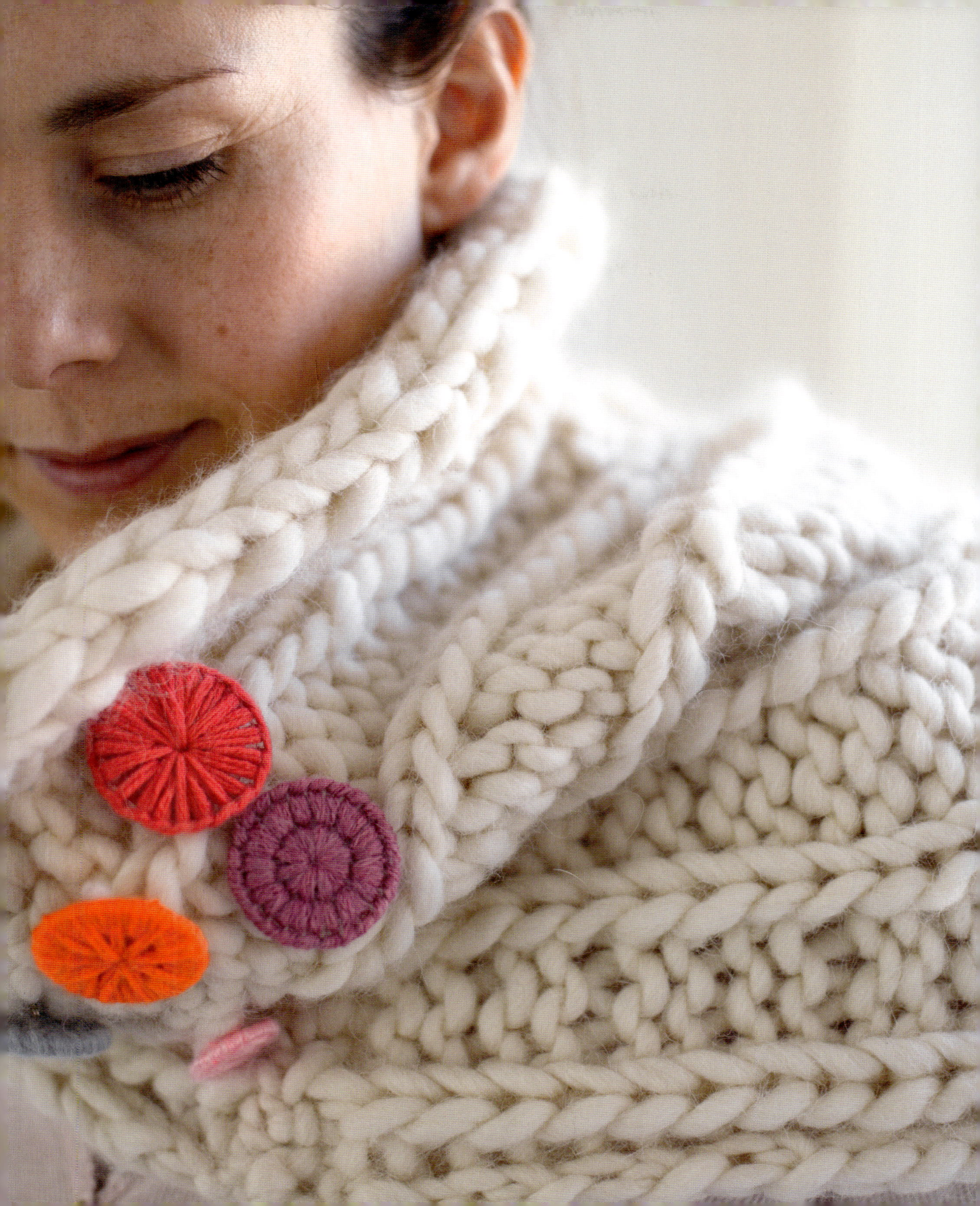

Wristbands

TIME 30 minutes

Moderate

SIZE Diameter approx. 5cm (2in), width 2–4cm (¾–1½in)

Materials

Yarn for mauve wristband
Rowan Wool Cotton, 50g in 977 (Frozen)

Yarn for pink wristband
Rowan Lima, 50g in 899 (Damask)
Work with two strands of yarn.

Yarn for lilac wristband
Rowan Lima, 50g in 901 (Violet)
Work with two strands of yarn.

Other items
4.5mm hook

Instructions for mauve wristband

Make a foundation chain (see p.90) of 25 ch.
Rounds 1–2: 2 ch, dc in each st, join with ss to second chain.
Round 3: For the bobble pattern: 3 ch (1 tr in first st of previous round, but do not finish the stitch, leaving 2 loops on hook; work 3 tr into same st, each time not finishing st; finally, draw loop through all 5 loops left on the hook. 1 ch, 1 dc in next st of previous round); rep pattern to end of round. Close round with 1 ss.
Round 4: 2 ch, dc in each st.
Round 5: 1 dc, dc2tog (see p.95); rep to end.

Instructions for pink wristband

Make a foundation chain (see p.90) of 36 ch. Work 36 dc around ring; join with 1 ss.
Round 1: Work dc, join with 1 ss, 2 ch.
Round 2: Work in tr, working 2 tr in every third st, 1 ss to join, 2 ch.
Round 3: RTRB (raised treble back: see p.94).
Round 4: Work in dc, working dc2tog in every third and fourth st (see p.95).
Round 5: Work in ss.

Instructions for lilac wristband

Make a foundation chain (see p.90) of 30 ch.
Round 1: Work in dc.
Round 2: Work in ss, but only insert hook into the back loop, 3 ch.
Round 3: Tr3tog in first st (that is, work 1 tr in first st of previous round, but do not finish st, leaving 2 loops on the hook; work second and third tr into same st, again not completing the stitch; there are now 4 loops on the hook, draw through all loops to finish), (1 ch, tr3tog in next st but one); rep pattern to end. 1 ss to join, 3 ch.
Round 4: Tr3tog in next ch space of previous round, 1 ch; rep to end.
Round 5: Work 1 dc in each ch space and each tr3tog of previous round.
Round 6: Work in ss.

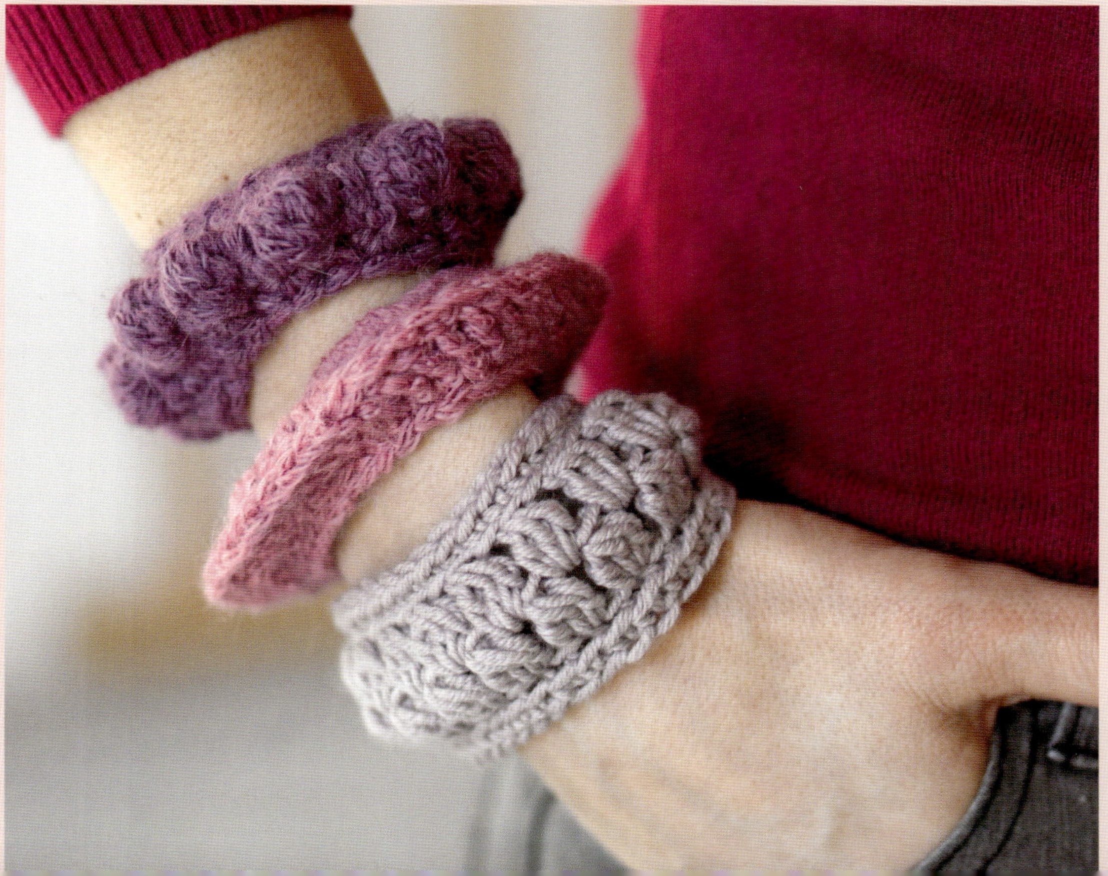

Headband

TIME 1 hour

Easy

SIZE Width 10cm (4in), adjustable to fit any head

Materials

Yarn

Schachenmayr original Merino Super Big Mix, 100g in 00036 (pink)

Other items

1 pair of 7mm (UK2/US10½) needles

Instructions

Cast on 12 stitches, then work in rows as follows:
Row 1: K1, (k1, p1) to last st, k1.
Row 2: K1, p1.
These two rows form the pattern. Rep pattern until you have the desired head size, then cast off. Graft the ends of the strip together (see p.89) to make the headband.

For the "belt", cast on 7 stitches and knit in stocking stitch. Work approx. 14cm (5½in), then cast off. Place the belt inside out around the seam of the headband and graft together (see p.89). Turn the belt right side out, with the seam to the inside.

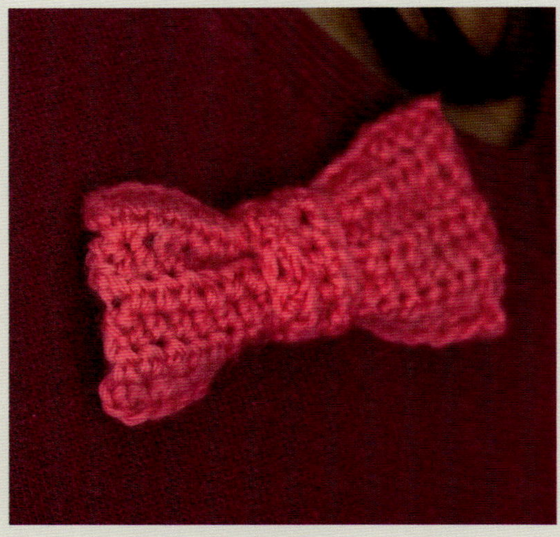

*This bow brooch in pink is also gathered in the middle with a belt. It was worked in Schachenmayr Baby Wool with a 3mm hook. Work 20 ch.
Row 1: Htr starting at third chain from hook, turn.
Rows 2–7: 2 ch, htr. Fasten off.
For the belt, work a chain of 10 ch, join in a ring.
Work in rounds as for rows 1 and 2 above.
Round 3: 1 ch, dc to end. Sew together in a loop.
Pull the rectangle through the belt and fasten a brooch pin on the back.*

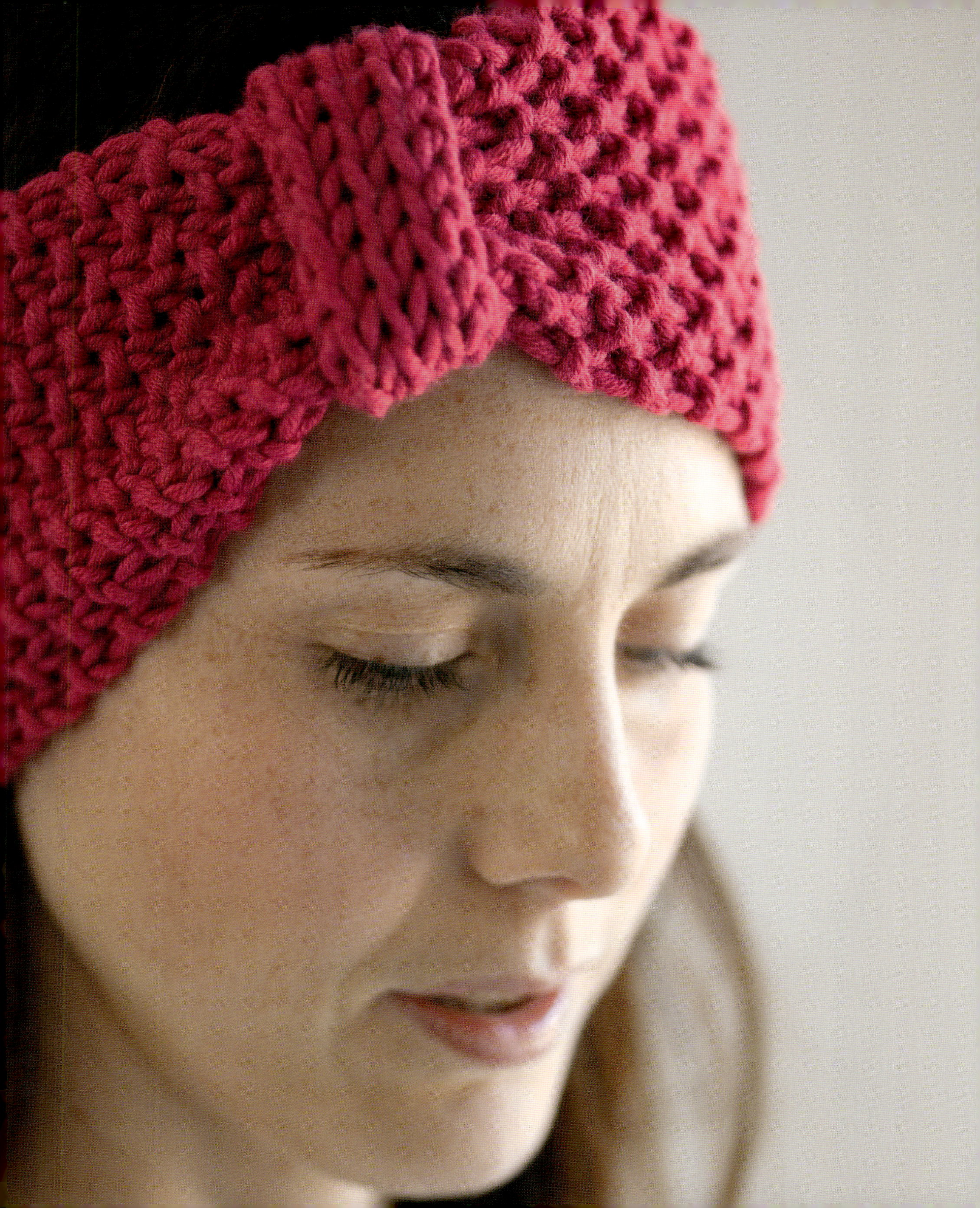

Tubular necklaces

TIME 3 hours each

Moderate

SIZE Adjustable

Materials

Yarn

Rowan Wool Cotton, 50g each in 977 (Frozen) and 900 (Antique)

Other items

4 x 3.5mm (UK9/US4) double-pointed needles

40 cotton wool balls (diameter: 2.5cm/1in)

Chain and 2 eyelets

Instructions for mauve necklace

Cast on 10 stitches, and divide them over three needles. Work in rounds in purl until the necklace measures approx. 60cm (23½in). Close one end firmly and insert a few cotton balls. Close other end in the same way. Insert eyelets into each end of the necklace and attach the chain to them.

Instructions for white necklace

For the white necklace cast on 14 stitches. Divide the stitches over three needles. Knit in rounds until the tube measures approx. 1m (39in). Cast off. Cut the yarn, leaving a tail 2½ times the length of the necklace; thread it through the cast-off stitches with a needle and pull tightly.

Insert the first cotton ball into the tube, run the long yarn tail along the outside of the necklace, and tie a knot after the cotton ball. Push in the next cotton ball, run the yarn along, and make another knot as before. Continue until the necklace is filled with cotton balls. Sew together both ends.

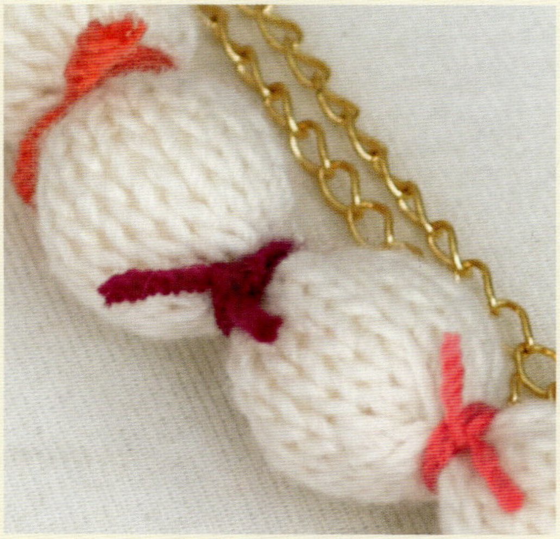

Colourful ends of yarn tied between some of the cotton balls add a pretty touch.

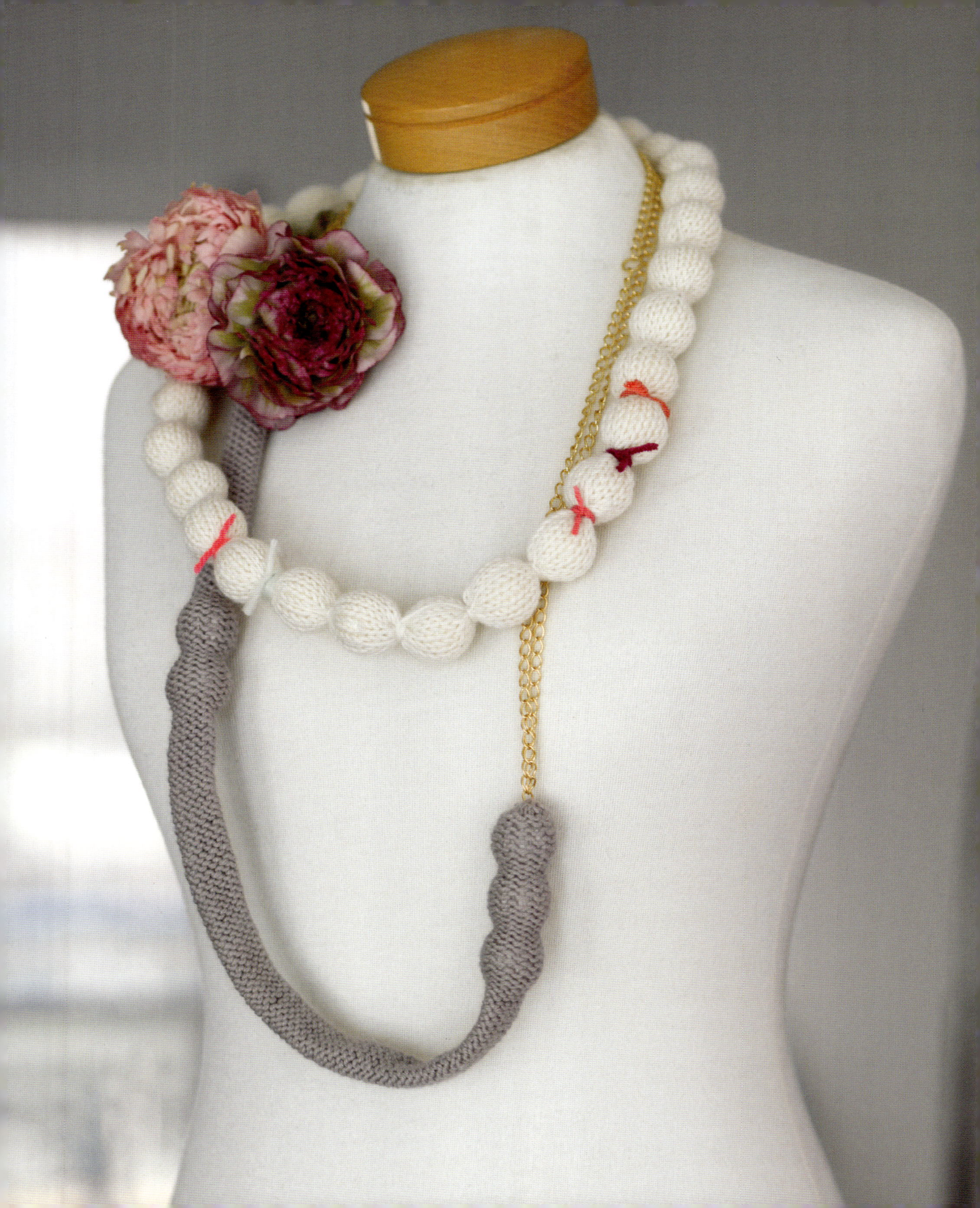

Bolero waistcoat

TIME Approx. 2 hours

Moderate

SIZE Clothing sizes
UK 8–12 (36–40)

Materials

Yarn

Rowan Big Wool, 300g in 058 (Heather)
Work with two strands of yarn.

Other items

1 pair of 15mm (US19) needles (or, preferably, a circular one)
Wool cord, ribbon, or button for fastening

Instructions

This waistcoat is knitted in garter stitch, in one piece from bottom to top. Cast on 24 stitches.

Row 1: M1k after first and second st, and before last-but-one st and last st (see p.88). (28 sts)
Row 2: Knit, working M1k after first and before last st. (30 sts)
Rows 3–8: Rep rows 1 and 2. (48 sts)
Rows 9–10: As row 1. (56 sts)
Rows 11–12: As row 2. (60 sts)
Next 6 rows: K without further shaping.
Start right front armhole:
Row 1: S1, k1, psso, k1, pass previous stitch over, K13 and turn; leaving rem sts on needle.
Row 2: S1, k1, psso, k to end. (13 sts)
Row 3: S1, k1, psso, k1, pass previous stitch over, k10, turn. (11 sts)
Row 4: As row 2. (10 sts)
Row 5: S1, k1, psso, k to end. (9 sts)
Row 6: S1, k to end.
Rows 7–10: Rep rows 5 and 6. (7 sts)
Rows 11–16: S1, k to end.
Leave sts on needle; they are not used in foll rows.
Continue with the back, starting with new yarn at the bottom of the armhole.
Row 1: S1, k1, psso, K24, s1, k1, psso and turn, leaving rem 16 sts on needle.
Work 16 rows straight, slipping the first stitch of each row.

Next row: S1, k6, cast off knitwise for the neckline until only 7 sts remain. Leave these stitches on the needle.
Work left front side in the same way as the right. Start again with a new yarn at the outer edge, with the first row and with the inside of the bolero facing you. This means the second side must be worked in purl to make the outside look like garter st.
Graft the shoulder seams (still on needle) together with Kitchener stitch (see p.24).

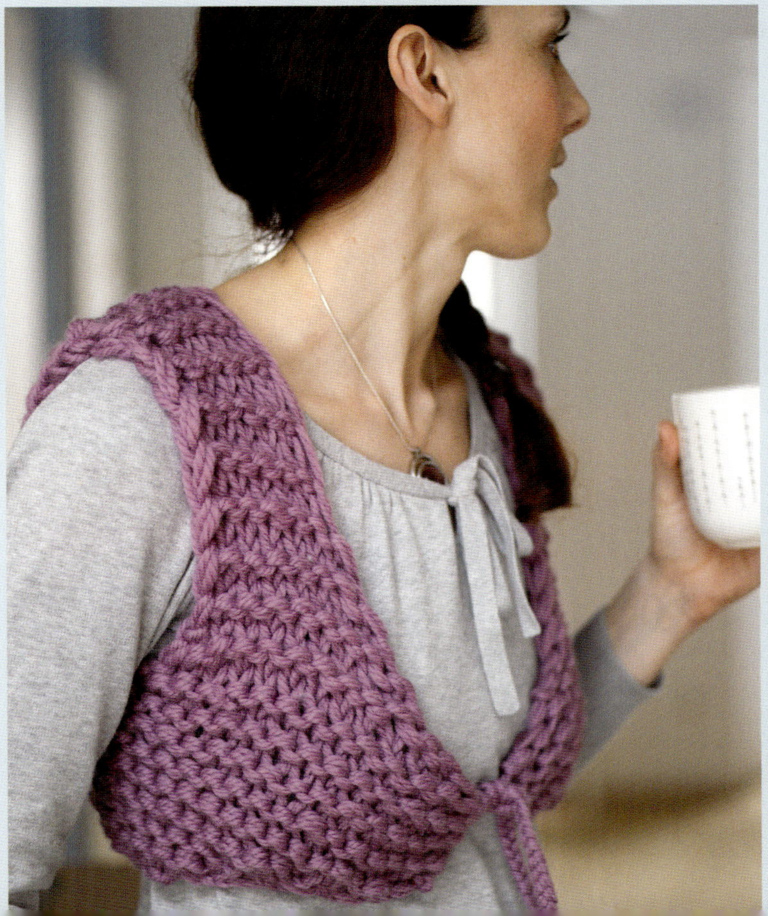

Attach a wool cord, ribbon, or button to the front sides of the bolero waistcoat to fasten.

Slippers

TIME	1½ hours
	Moderate
SIZE	Adapt to fit

Materials

Yarn for pink slippers
Schachenmayr select Apiretto, 100g in 08119 (powder)
Work with two strands of yarn.

Yarn for grey slippers
Schachenmayr select Benevito, 100g in 01316 (light grey)

Yarn for jade slippers
Schachenmayr original Bravo Big, 200g in 00170 (jade)

All the soles are worked in Schachenmayr original Bravo Big, as it is a hard-wearing yarn.

Other items
6mm hook

Instructions

Make a foundation chain (see p.90): it should be the same length as the sole, minus the width of the sole at its widest point. Add 3 ch.
Round 1: Tr in each ch, starting with fourth ch from hook and working 6 tr in last st. Work back along the other side of the chain in tr, 6 tr in first st of foundation chain, end with 1 ss in first tr.

Continue in rounds as follows:
Round 2: 2 ch, tr to end. You have to increase at four points in this round, at the four "corners" of the foot: each time, work 3 tr in a st of previous round. Close round with 1 ss in first stitch of previous round.

This completes the sole of the slipper. If you like, you can now change colour or even change yarn.
Round 3: 2 ch, RTRB (raised treble back) to end (see p.94). Finish round with 1 ss in first st of previous round.
Round 4: 2 ch, work in tr as far as the toe, tr2tog (Treble decrease, see p.95), 1 tr, tr2tog, 1 tr, tr3tog, tr to end, finish with 1 ss in first st of previous round.
Round 5: 2 ch, work in tr, tr6tog at toe.
This completes the first slipper. Repeat for second slipper.

Variation

For the children's slippers, work half trebles instead of trebles.

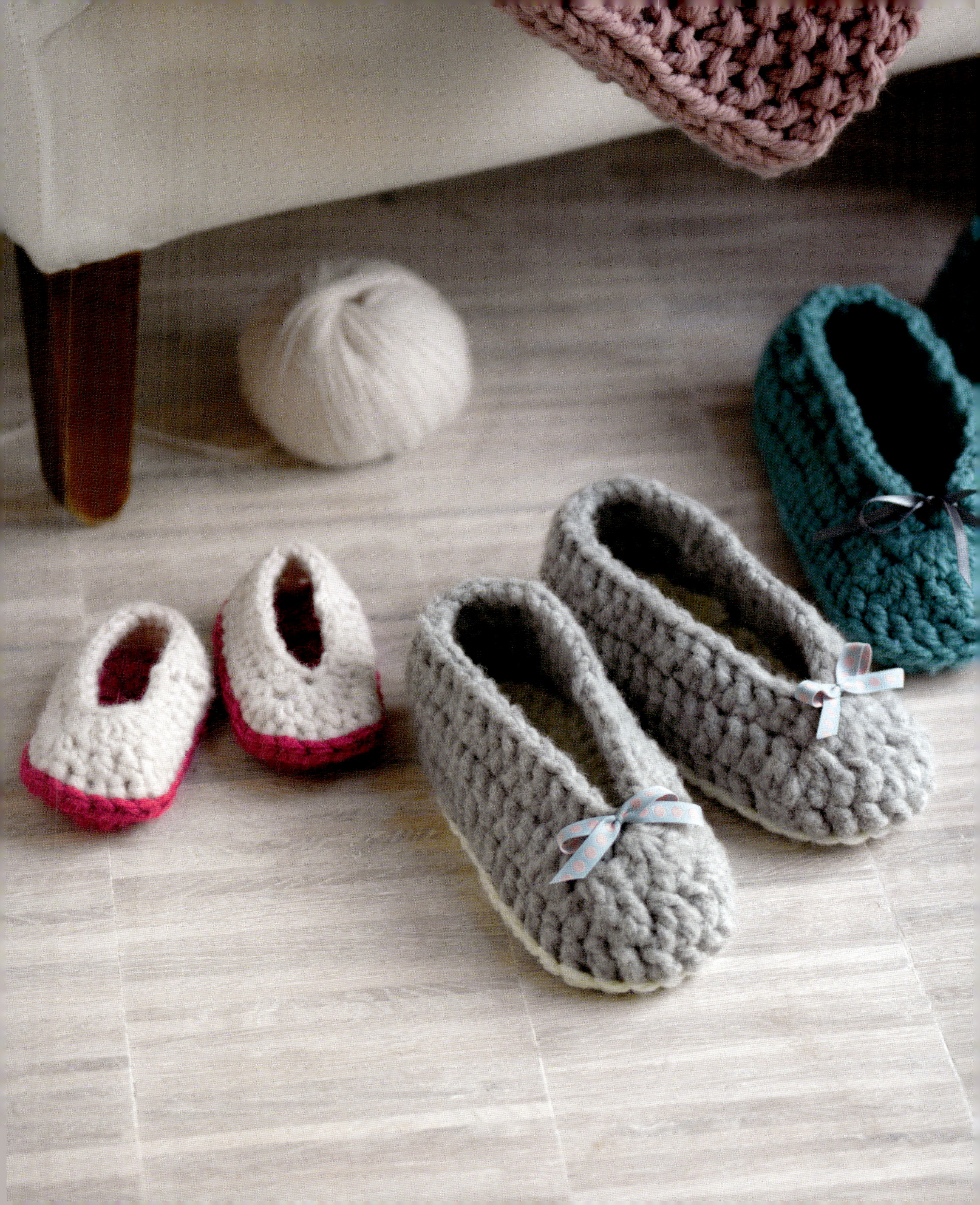

Quick guide to knitting and crocheting

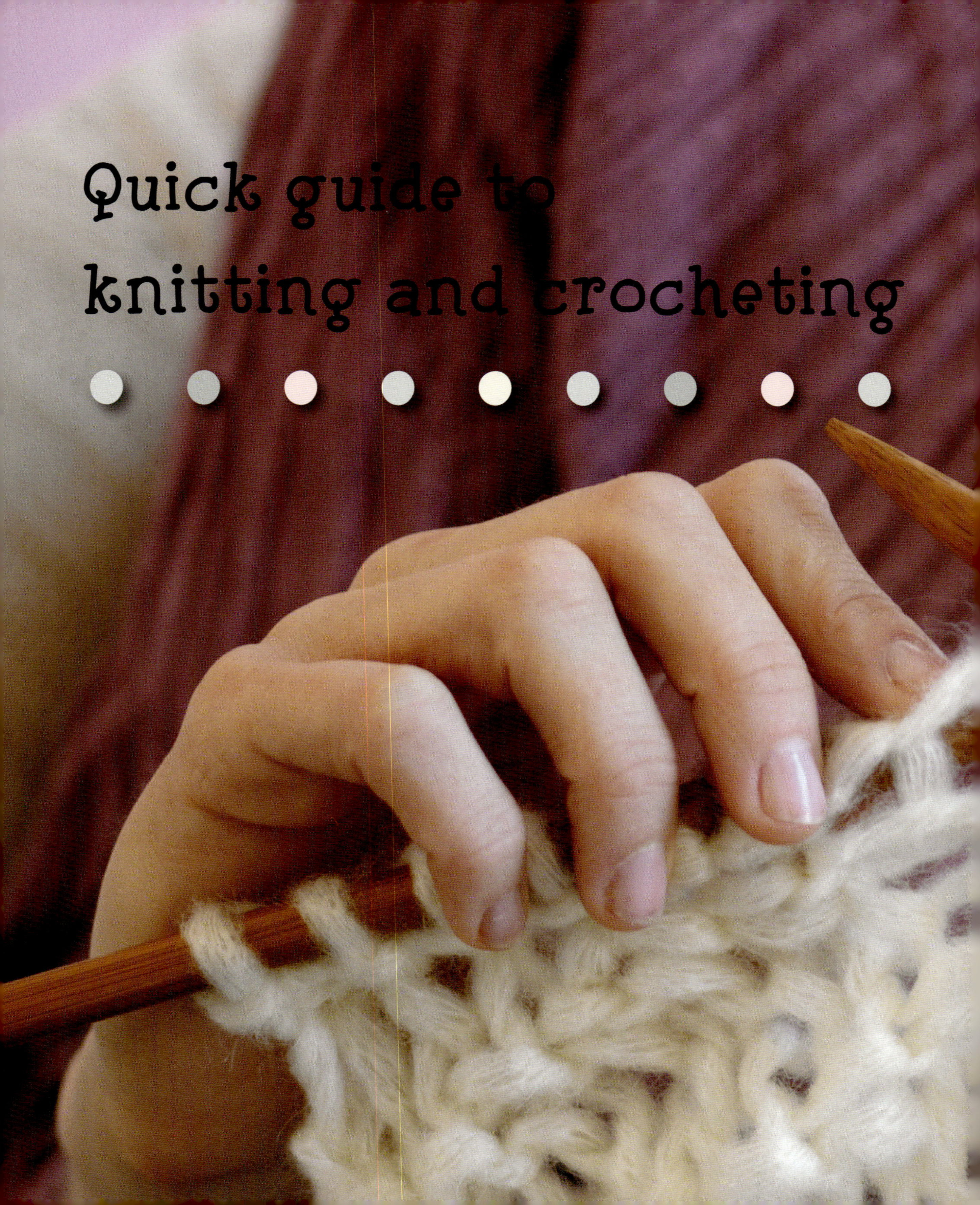

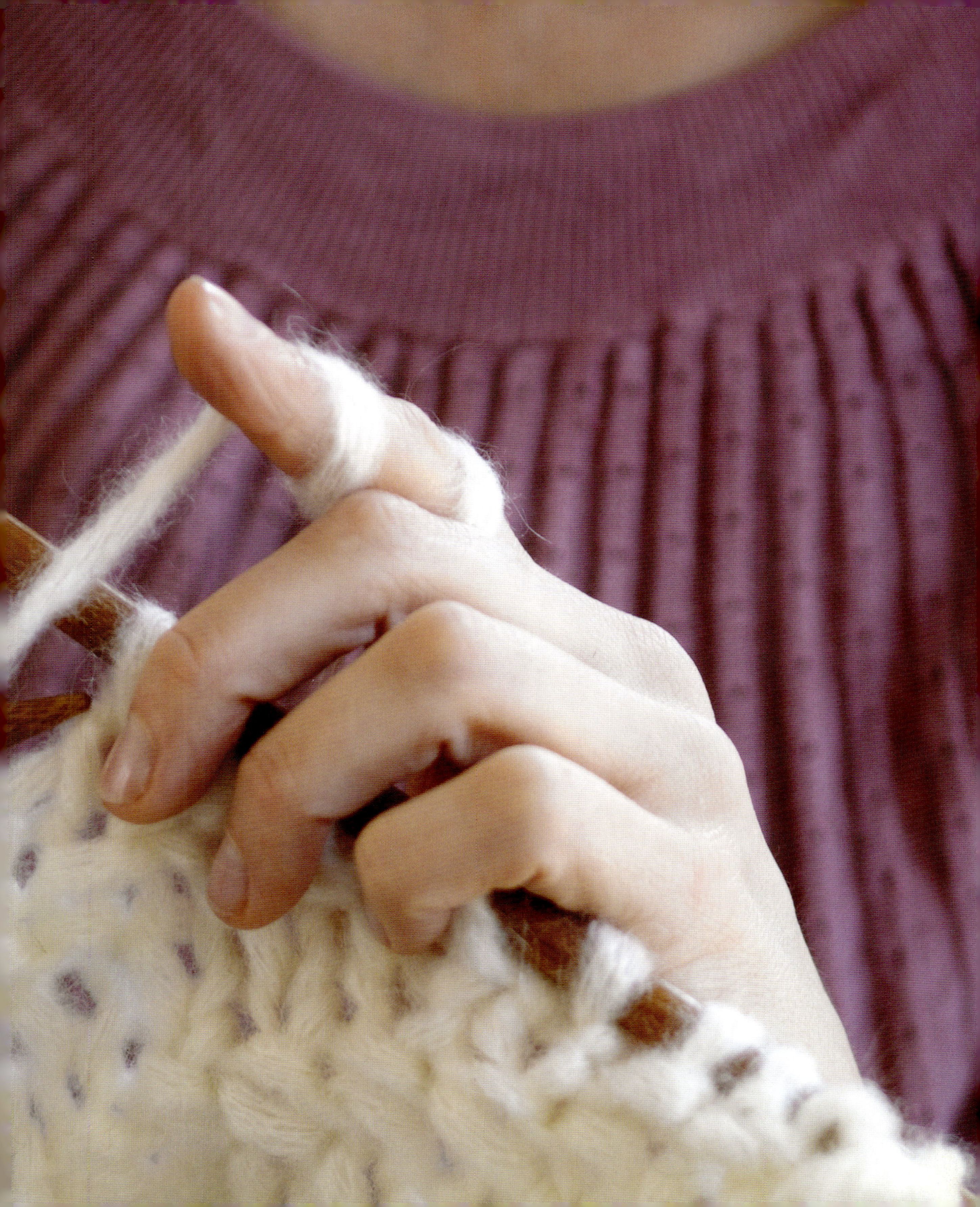

Double cast-on

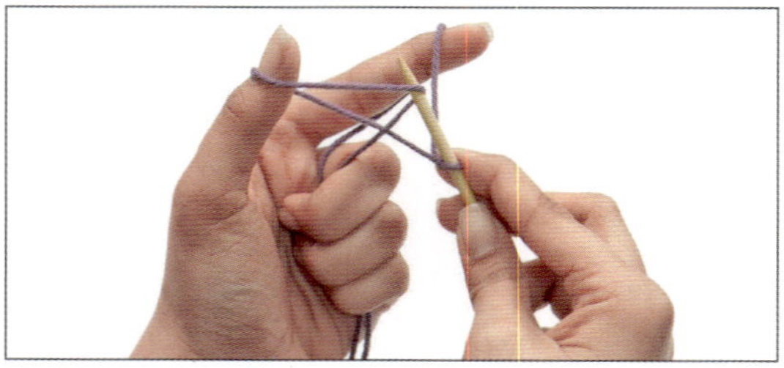

1. Make a slip knot, leaving a long yarn tail – approx. 3.5cm (1⅜in) per stitch. Holding the needle in your right hand, loop the working yarn over your left thumb and the yarn tail over your forefinger. Hold the ends in place with your other fingers. Then bring the needle under and up through the thumb loop.

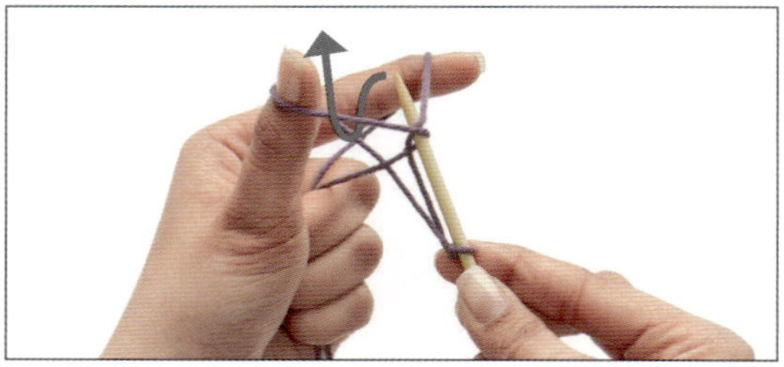

2. Wrap the needle around the loop on your forefinger from right to left, and pull the loop you have formed down under the thumb yarn and through in the direction of the arrow.

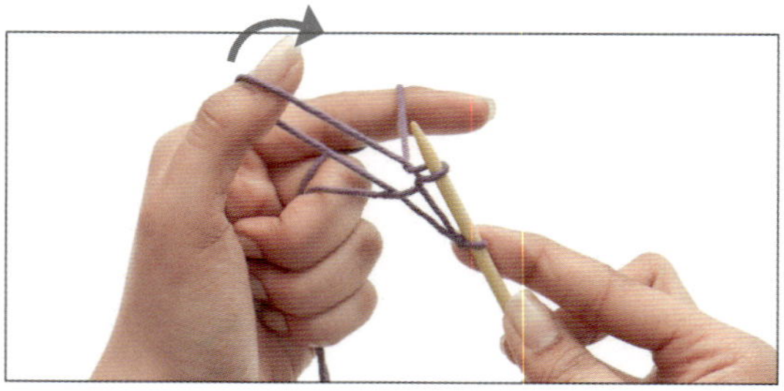

3. Draw your thumb out of the loop.

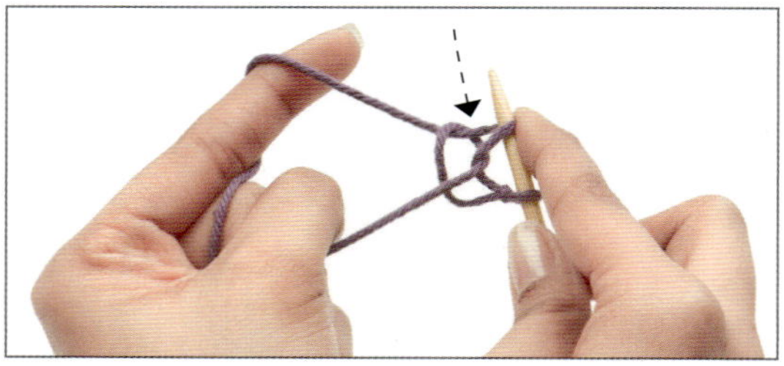

4. Slide the loop onto the needle beside the slip knot and tighten it gently – the second stitch is complete.

Provisional (or contrast-edge) cast-on

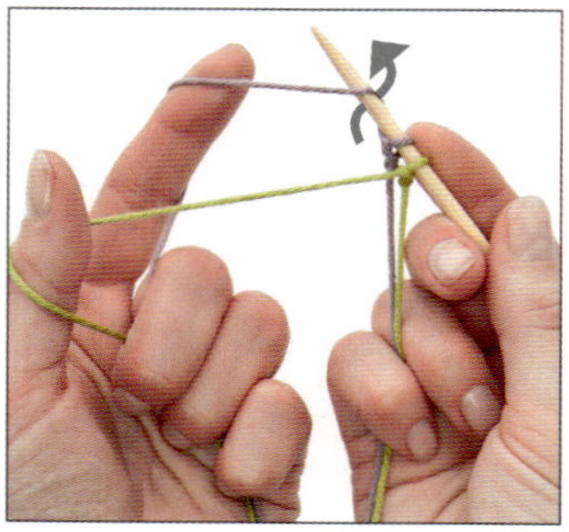

1. Make a slip knot in the end of a contrasting colour of yarn (shown here in green). It should be twice the length of the proposed edge. Place it on the needle.

2. Make a slip knot in the main yarn as well, and place it on the needle.

3. Hold the strands as for casting on. The contrasting yarn goes around the thumb.

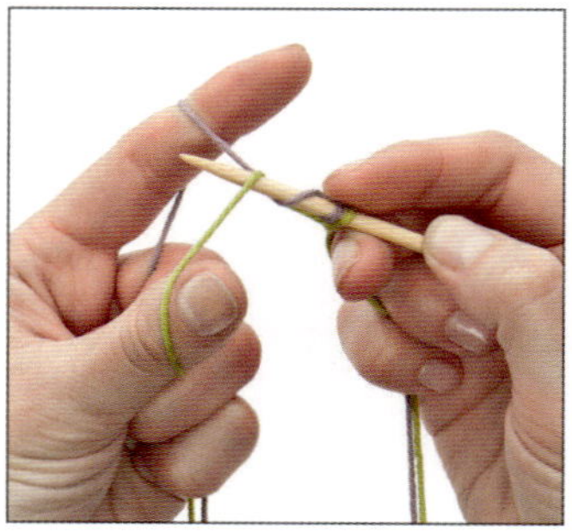

4. Bring the needle down between the yarns and draw it up and under the main yarn (see arrow on the photo far left).

5. Bring the needle towards you over the contrasting yarn, then under and away from you again.

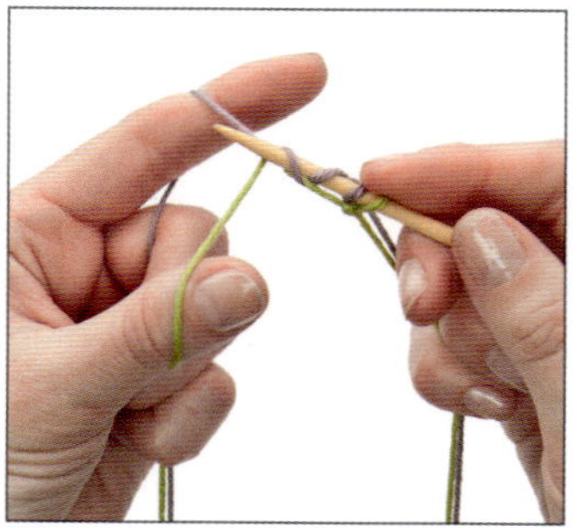

6. Wrap the main yarn around the needle from the top and back, and draw it under and through the contrasting yarn. Slide the contrasting yarn back onto the needle. Repeat steps 4–6 until you have the desired number of stitches.

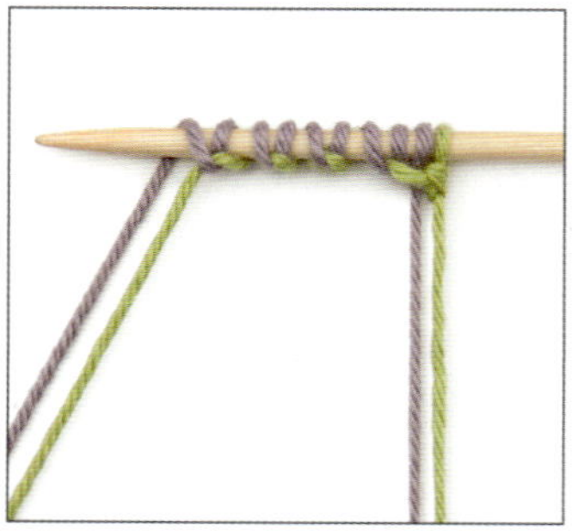

7. Remove the contrasting slip knot from the needle at the end of the cast-on row. Tie the strands together. When knitting the first row, insert the needle into the front of the stitches. You can remove the contrasting yarn later when you want to pick up the "live" stitches from the start of the work.

Knit stitch

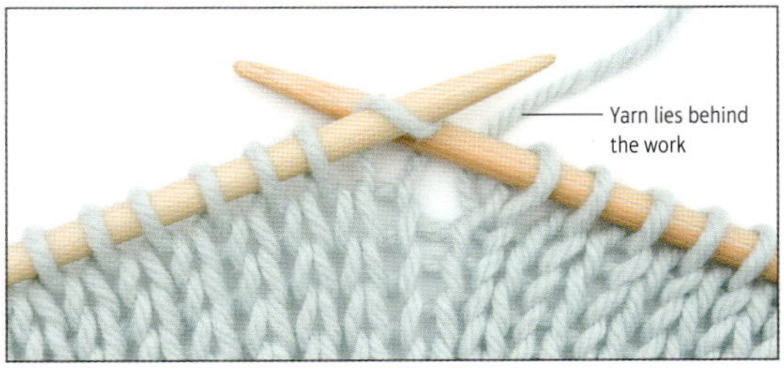

1. The knitted stitches always sit on the right needle. The yarn lies behind the work. Insert right needle into first stitch on left needle from front to back.

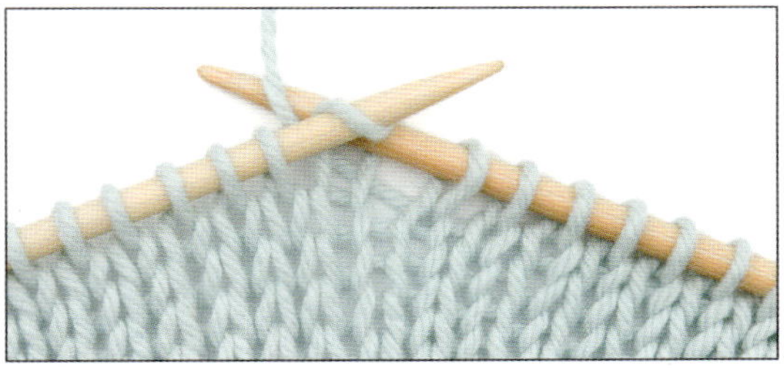

2. Wrap the yarn under and around needle. Make sure the yarn is kept at an even tension.

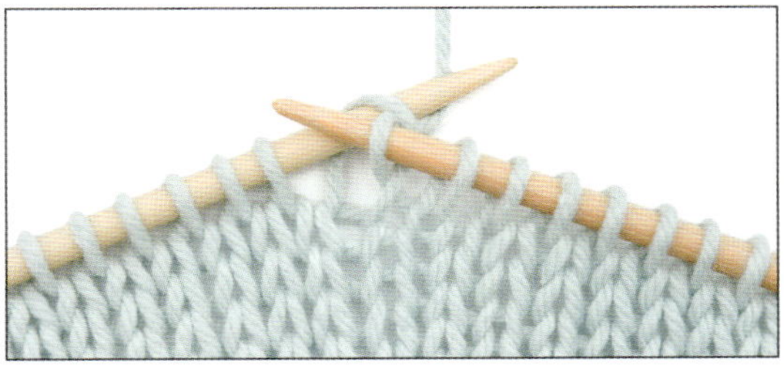

3. Catch the yarn firmly with the right needle and draw it through the stitch on the left needle. When you do this, don't hold the yarn either too tightly or too loosely.

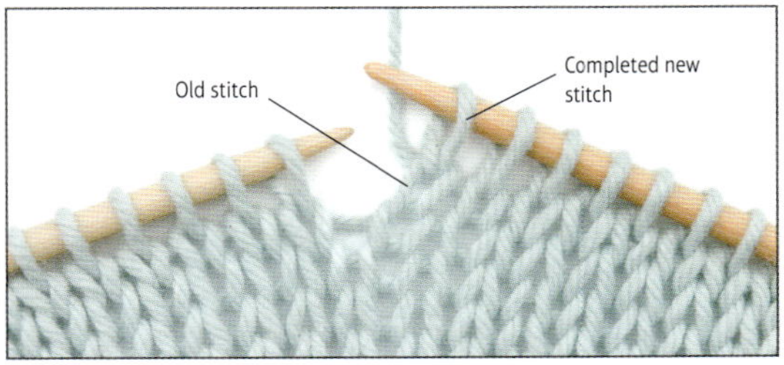

4. Slide the old stitch off the left needle. Knit every stitch in the same way to the end of the row. When all the stitches are on the right needle, turn the work and hold it with your left hand.

Purl stitch

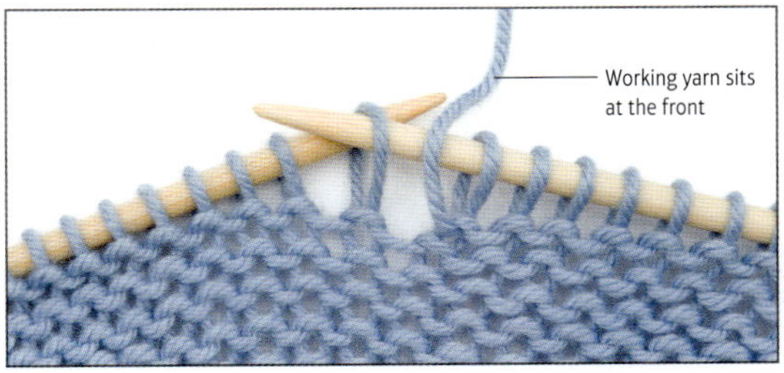

1. The yarn sits in front of the work. From behind, insert the right needle forwards into the first stitch on the left needle.

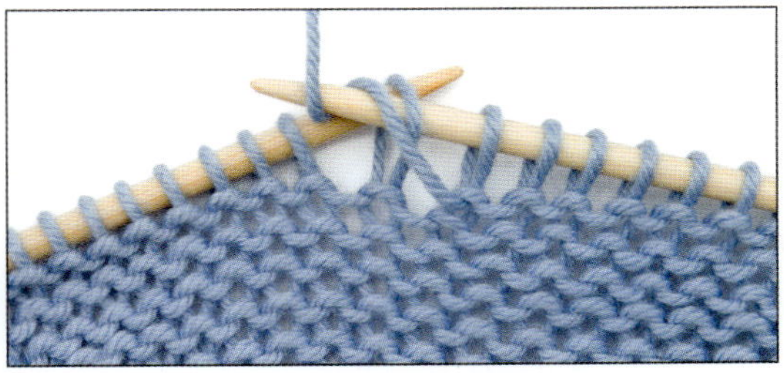

2. Wrap the yarn around the tip of the right needle from front to back. Make sure to keep an even tension on the yarn.

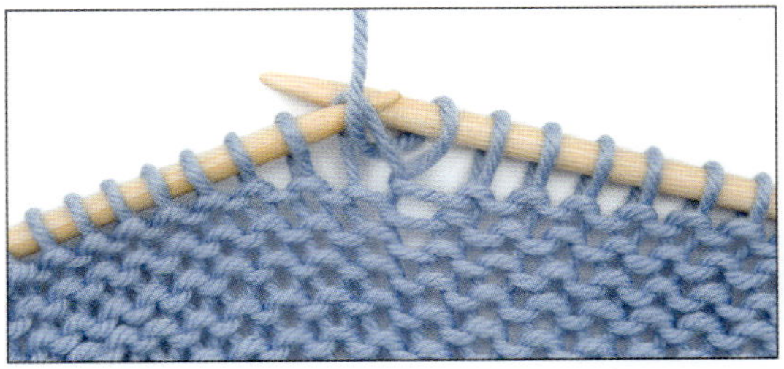

3. Draw the yarn through the stitch with the right needle, from front to back. Keep your hands relaxed, moving slowly and steadily.

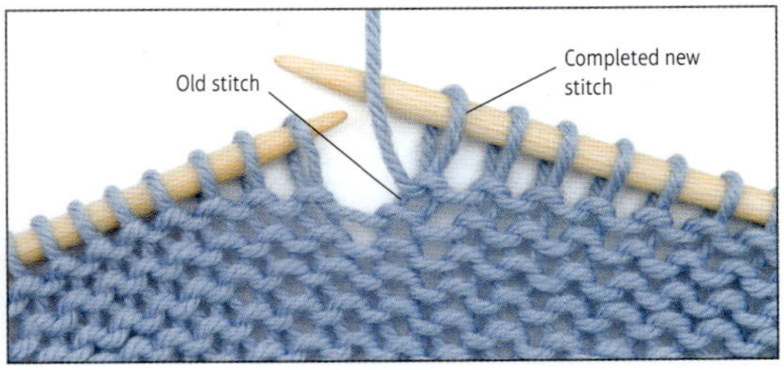

4. Slide the old stitch off the left needle. Work every stitch in the same way to the end of the row. When all the stitches are on the right needle, turn the work and hold it with your left hand.

Make 1 left-cross increase

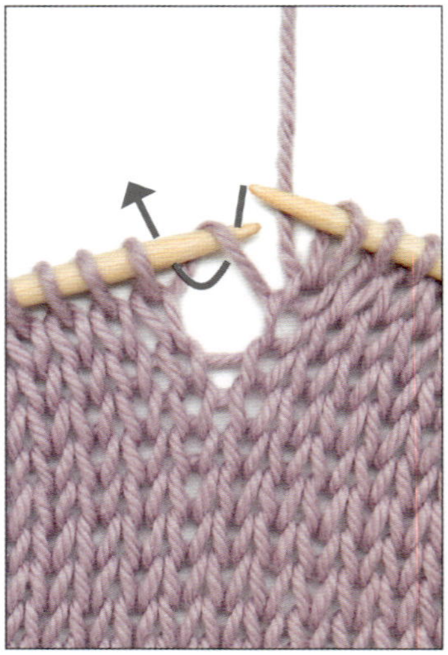

1. With the left needle, lift up the horizontal strand between the stitch just knitted and the next one, as shown.

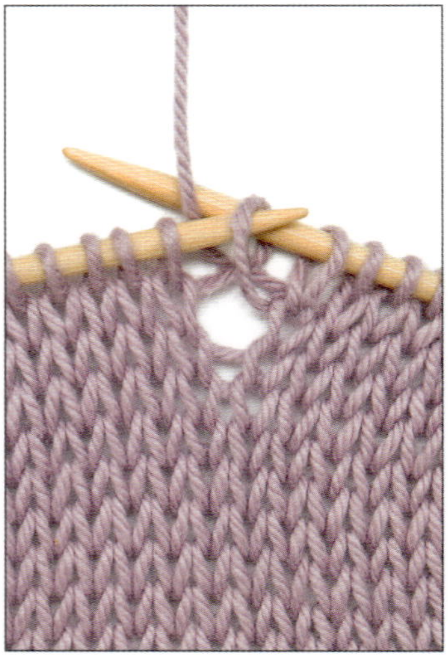

2. Then insert right needle into the back of the lifted loop, wrap working the yarn around the needle, and draw it through the lifted loop.

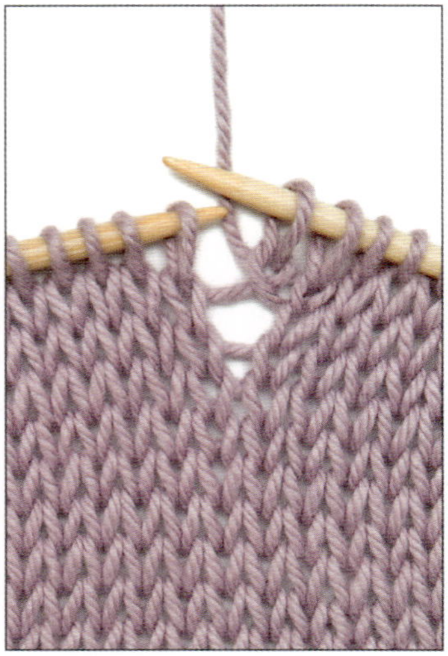

3. This twists the loop to the left at the base of the new stitch, so there is no visible hole in the knitted work.

This stitch is used each time to increase at the end of the row in the Bolero pattern (left-leaning increase). At the start of the row you need a right-leaning increase: for this, you lift the horizontal bar onto the left needle from back to front, then insert the right needle from left to right into the front of the loop, and knit a stitch as normal.

Cast off

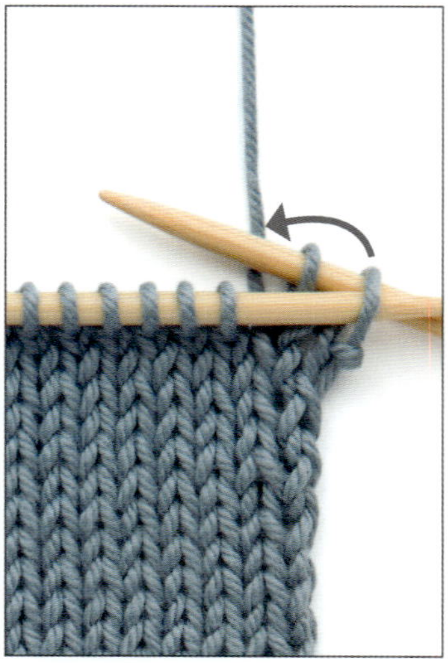

1. Knit the first two stitches. Then insert the left needle into the first stitch and lift it up and over the second one.

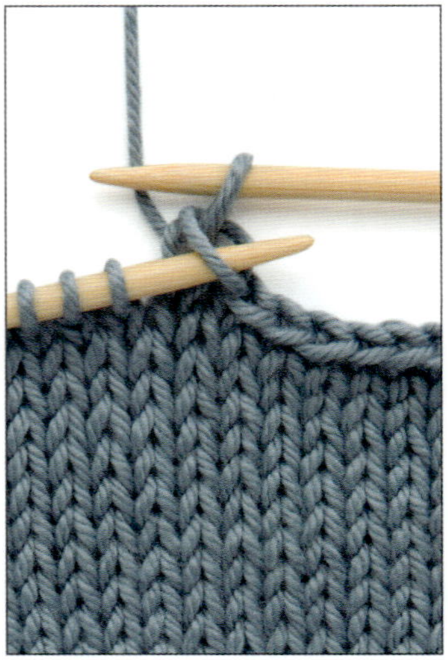

2. Knit another stitch and lift the previous one over it. Repeat until only one stitch is left on the needle.

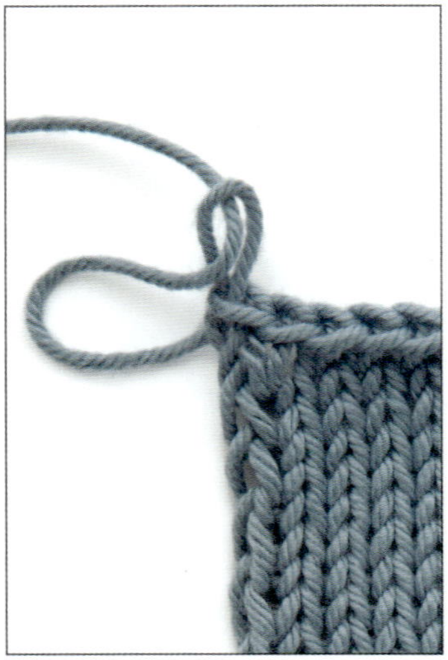

3. Cut the yarn, leaving approx. 20cm (8in), long enough to sew in the end neatly, or leave a much longer yarn tail to use later for a seam. Pass the yarn tail through the remaining stitch.

Grafting

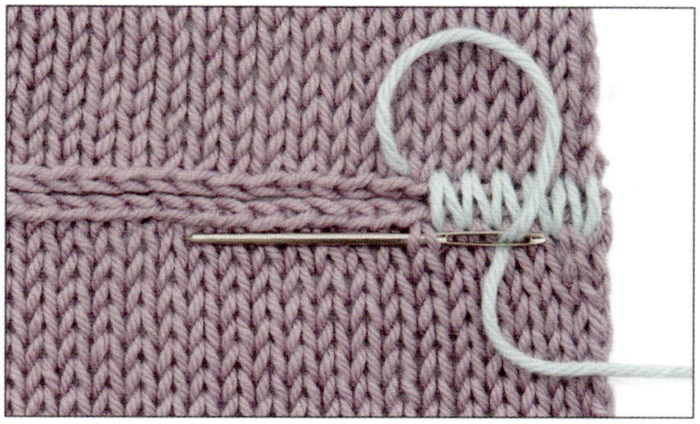

1. Align the pieces edge to edge with the right sides facing you. Sew from right to left through the stitches as shown. The sewing yarn runs like a knitted stitch.

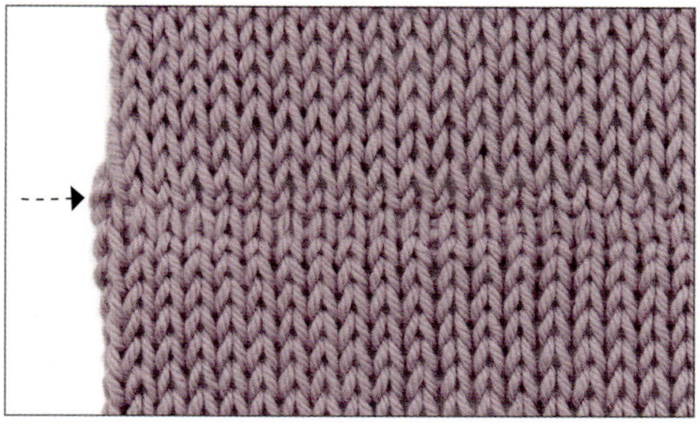

2. If you use the same knitting yarn for sewing up, the seam is almost invisible. The work looks like a continuous piece of knitting.

Mattress stitch

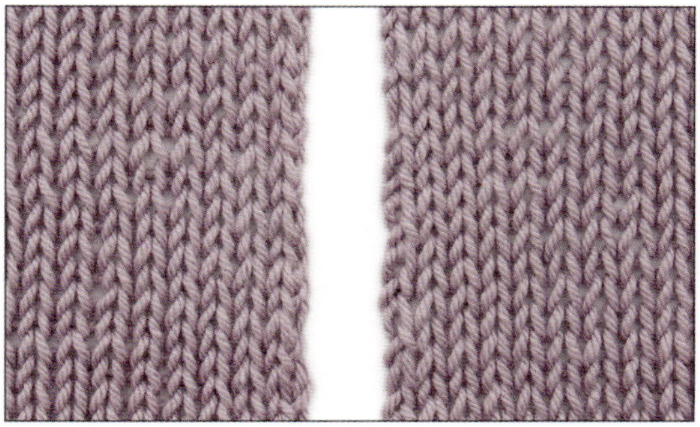

1. Mattress stitch is particularly good for joining wristbands and stocking stitch, creating a seam that is almost invisible. Align the two pieces alongside each other with both right sides facing.

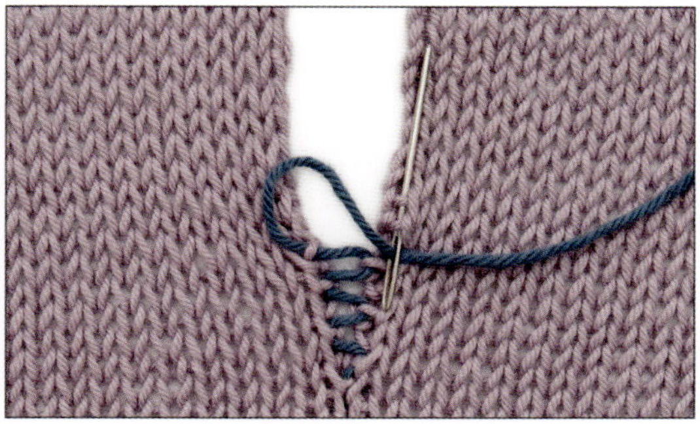

2. Insert the needle from front through the centre of the first stitch and then into the middle of the second stitch in the row above it. Repeat on the other side. Work up the seam, pulling the yarn together firmly.

Overcasting

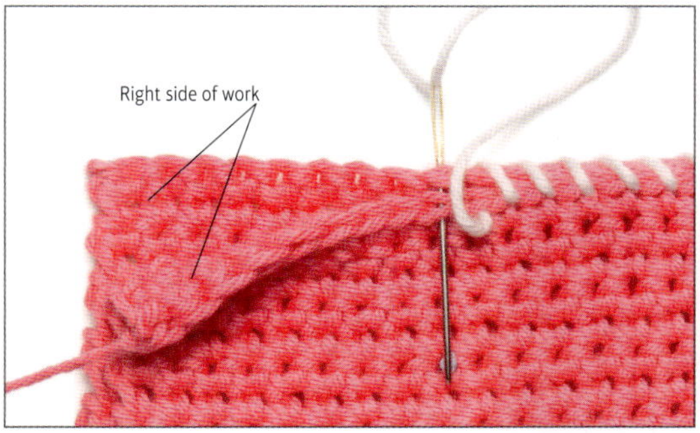

1. Simple overcast seam: align the pieces on top of each other, right sides together. Fasten the end of the yarn with two or three stitches. Work the yarn from back to front through both edges, inserting the needle right at the edge of the work.

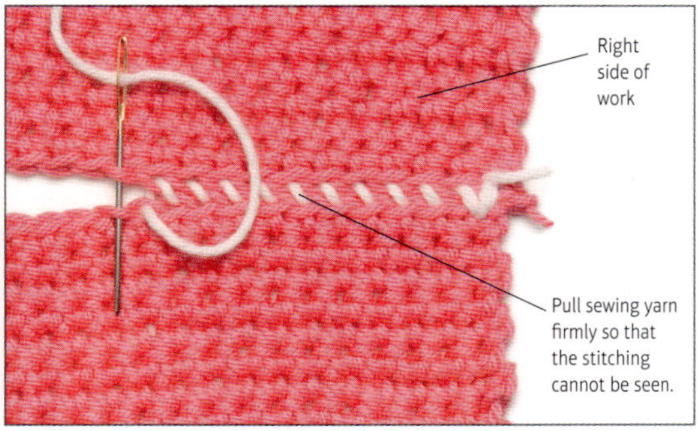

2. Flat overcast seam: if the seam needs to be completely flat, lay the edges alongside each other (right sides facing). Work in the same way as for the simple overcast seam, but only insert the needle through the top loop on both sides.

Foundation chain

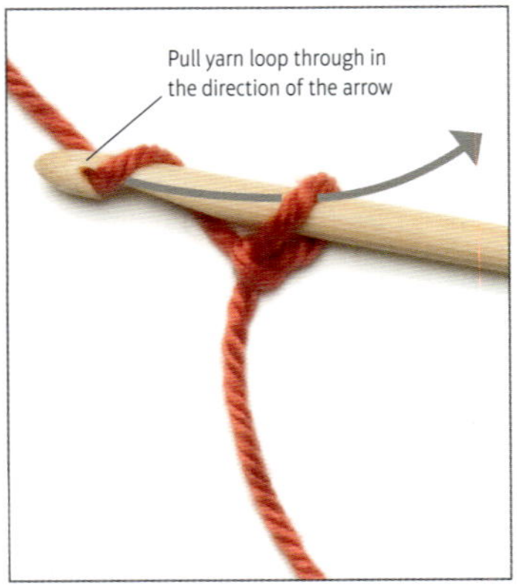

1. Make a slip knot. Wrap the yarn around the hook as shown here, and pull the hook through the stitch.

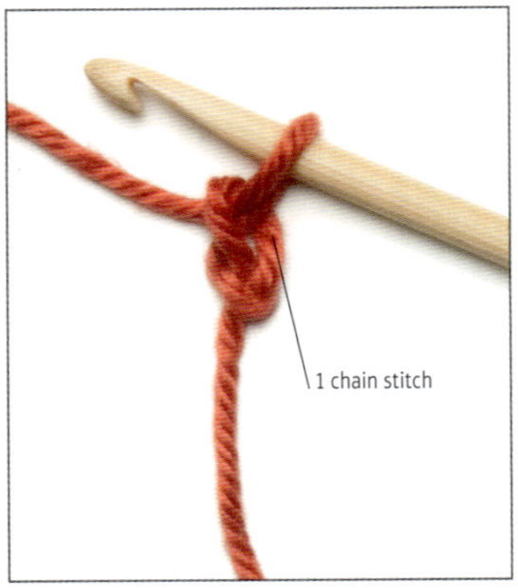

2. The first chain stitch is complete. Keep holding the loose yarn tail under the work with the other fingers of the yarn hand.

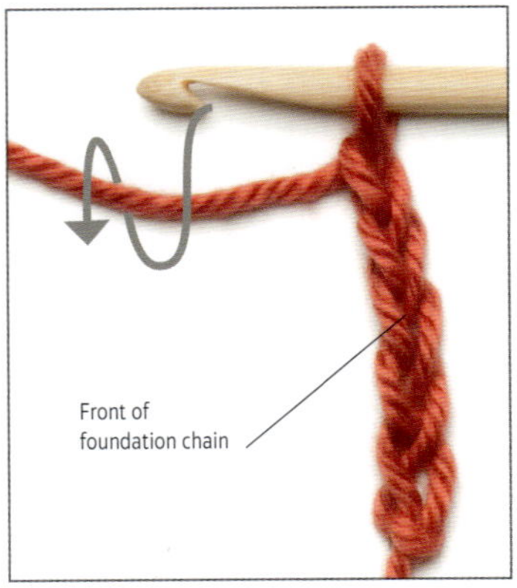

3. To make each following stitch, draw another loop through the stitch onto the hook. Continue until you have worked the desired number of chain stitches.

Slip stitches

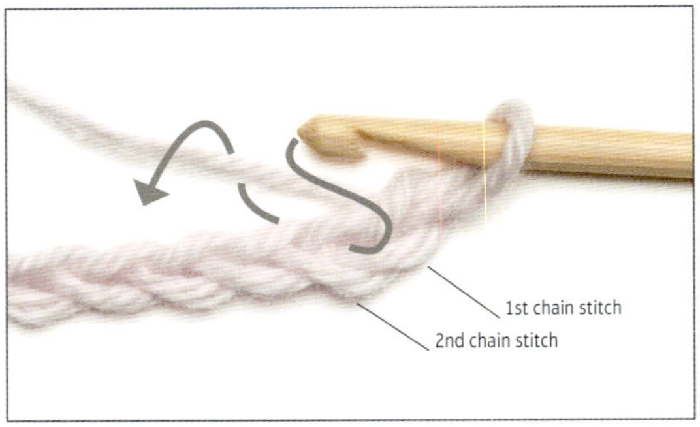

1. Start by working a foundation chain in the desired length. To make the first slip stitch, insert the hook through the second chain stitch (counting from the hook). There is only one strand of the chain stitch on the hook. Wrap the working yarn around the hook.

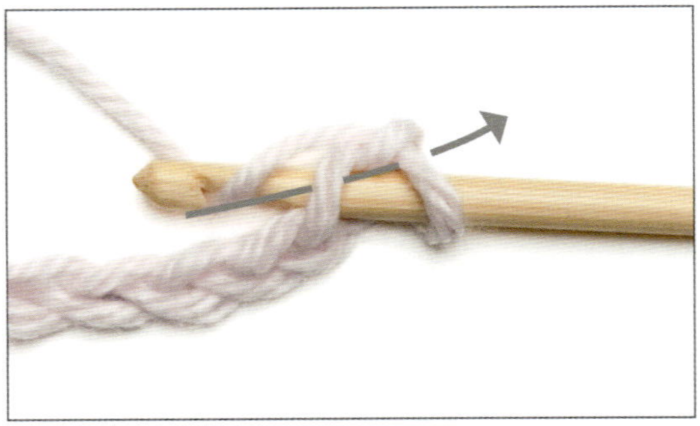

2. Hold the start of the foundation chain in place with your left hand. Keep the yarn taut. Pull the working yarn through the chain stitch with the hook in the direction of the arrow.

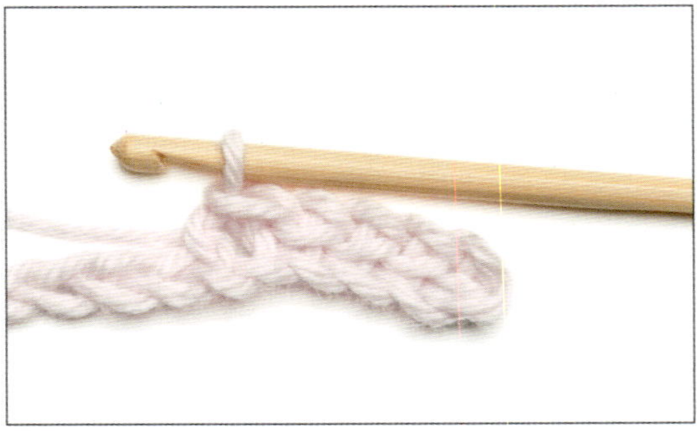

3. Work a slip stitch in all of the following chain stitches in the same way. Slip stitches should generally be worked quite loosely.

Closing chain stitches into a ring with a slip stitch

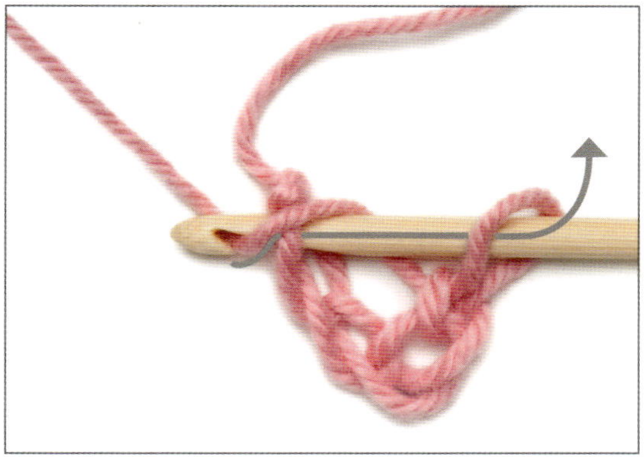

1. Slip stitches are used to close a ring for working in the round. Work the required number of chain stitches, then insert the hook into the first chain stitch. Wrap the yarn round, then pull the loop through the chain stitch and the stitch on the hook.

Double crochet

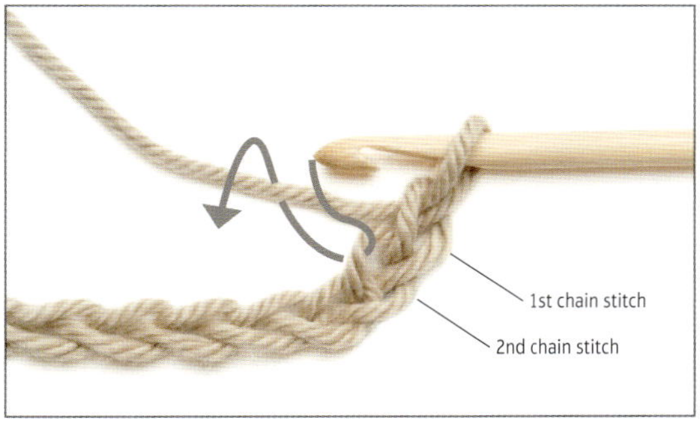

1. Work a foundation chain of the required length. Insert the hook into the second chain (counting from the hook) and pull through a yarn loop in the direction of the arrow. In this case the hook is inserted under one strand. From the next row on, the hook is inserted through two stitch loops of the previous row.

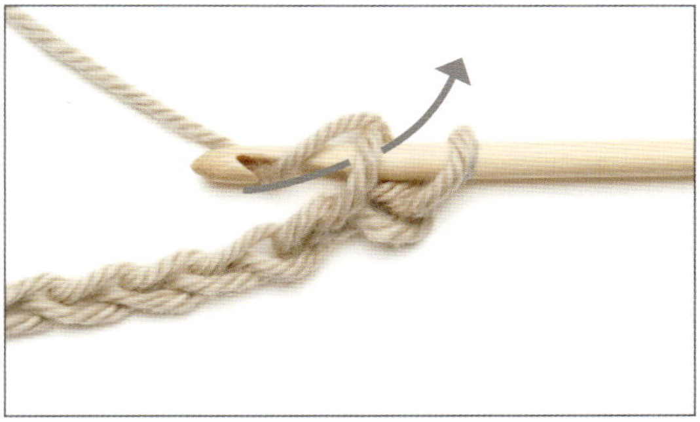

2. Hold the start of the foundation chain firmly with the left hand. Keep the yarn taut and pull a loop through the chain in the direction of the arrow.

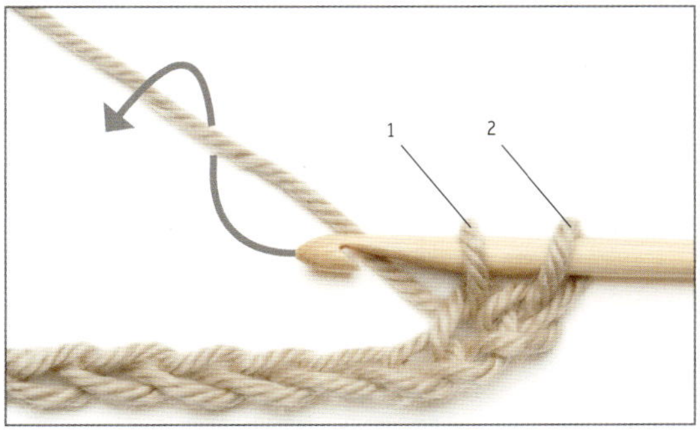

3. You now have two stitches on the hook. Wrap the hook around the yarn in the direction shown by the arrow.

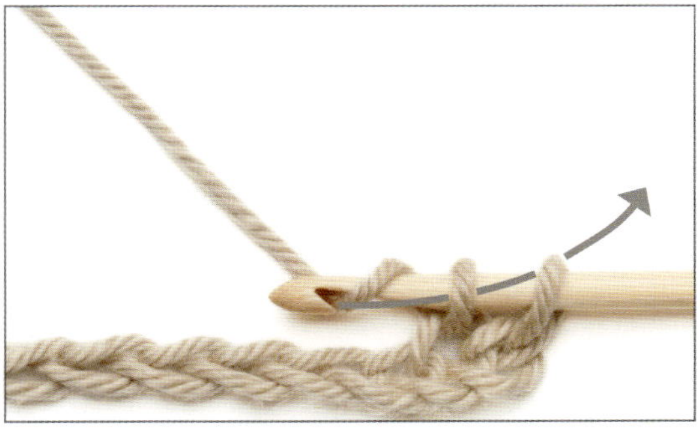

4. Draw the loop through the two stitches on the hook in one movement. As you do this, let the working yarn slip through your fingers while still keeping it taut.

Half treble

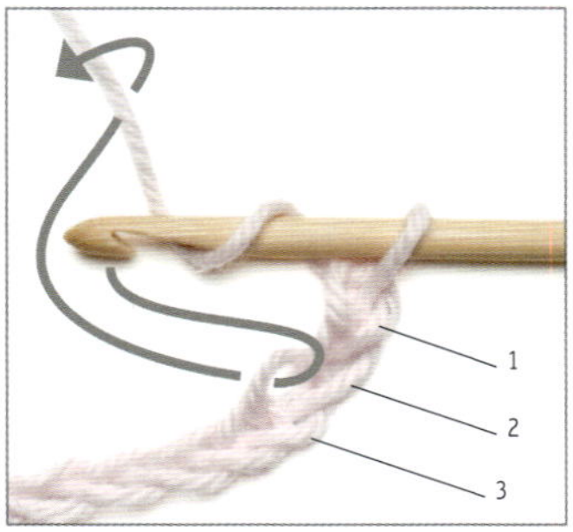

1. For the first half treble, wrap the yarn once around the hook. Insert the hook into the third stitch (counting from the hook) and draw a loop through the chain (see arrow).

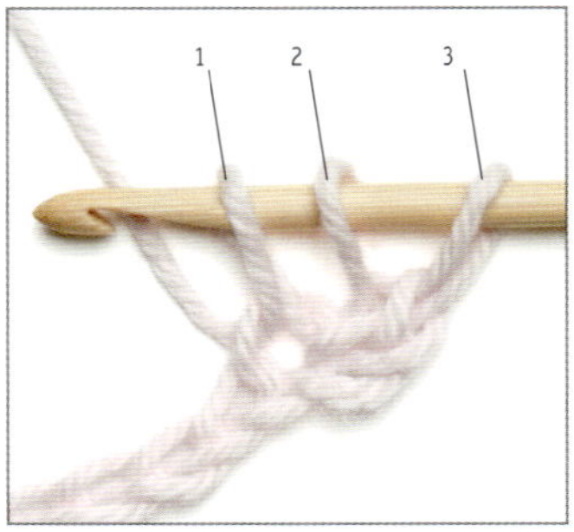

2. You now have three loops on the hook.

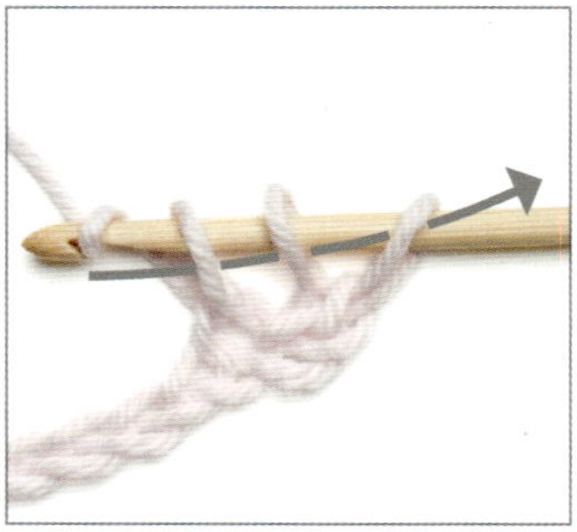

3. Draw the working strand through all three loops in one movement (see arrow). It takes a bit of practice to master this technique smoothly.

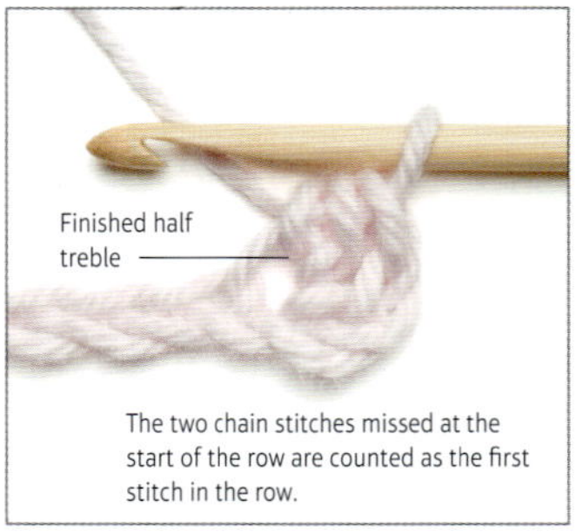

4. The first half treble is complete. Work the whole row in the same way. Turn, and start every following row with two chain stitches.

Treble

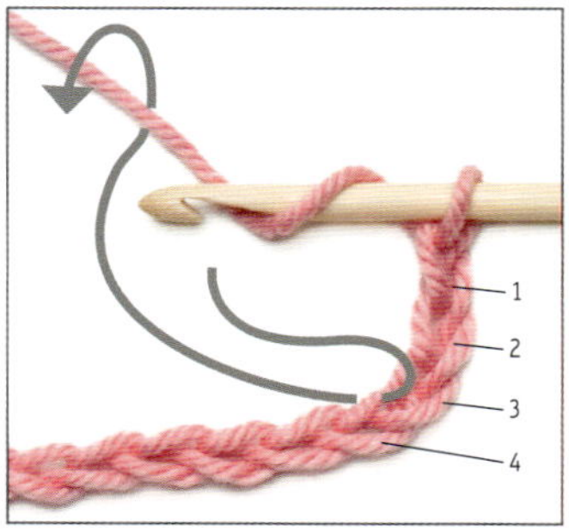

1. For the first treble, wrap the yarn once around the hook. Insert the hook into the fourth stitch (counting from the hook), catch the working yarn around the hook, and draw a loop through the chain (see arrow).

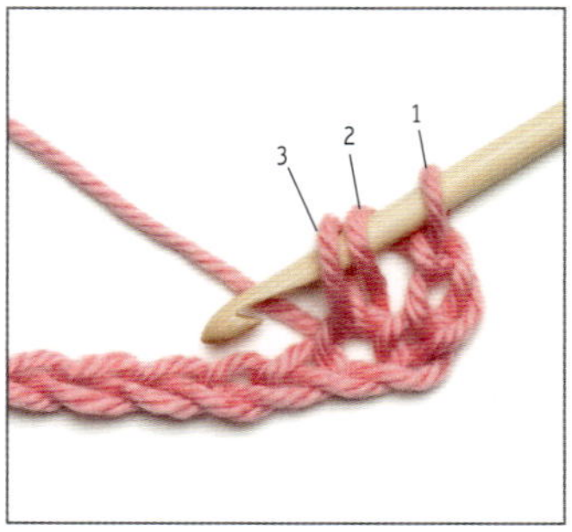

2. There are now three loops on the hook.

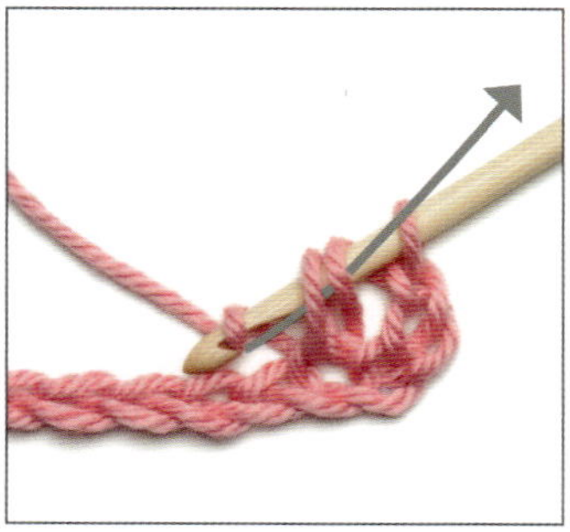

3. Catch the working yarn around the hook and draw it through the first two loops.

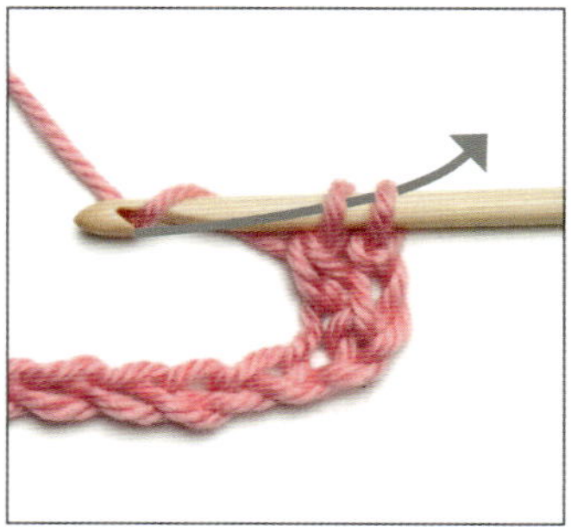

4. Now two loops are left on the hook. Catch the yarn again around the hook and draw it through both loops.

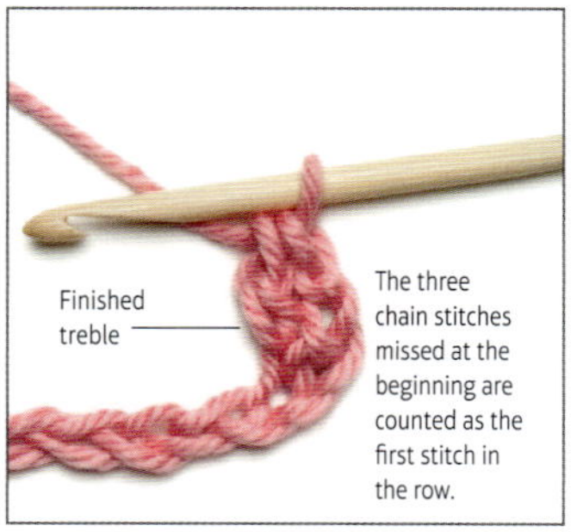

5. This completes the first treble. Start the following rows with two chain stitches.

Double treble

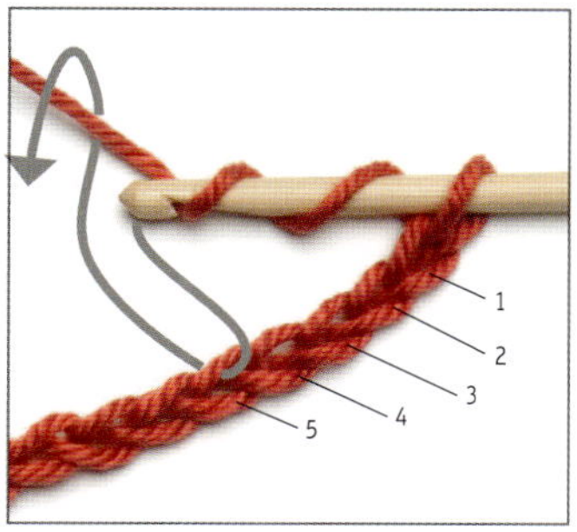

1. Work a foundation chain. Wrap the yarn twice around the hook. Insert the hook into the fifth chain (counting from hook). Catch the yarn around hook.

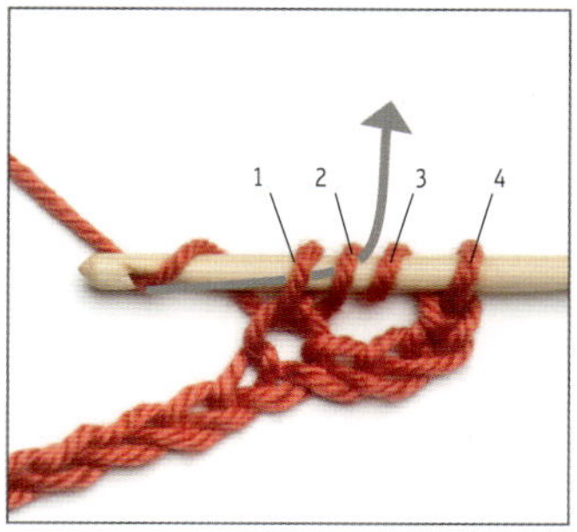

2. Draw a loop through the chain. Now there are four loops on the hook. Draw the yarn through the first two loops on the hook.

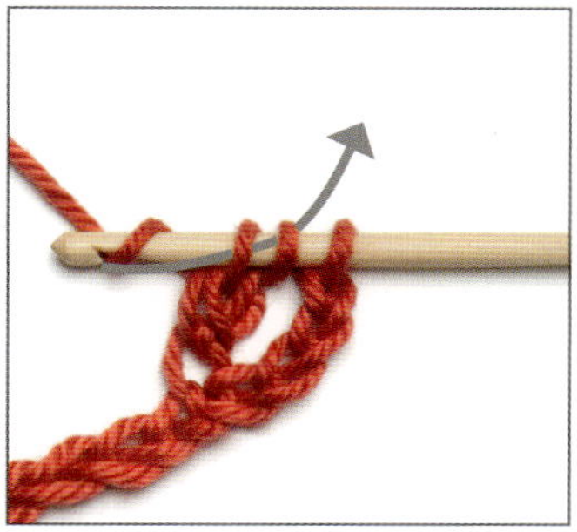

3. Three loops are left. Draw the yarn through the first two loops on the hook.

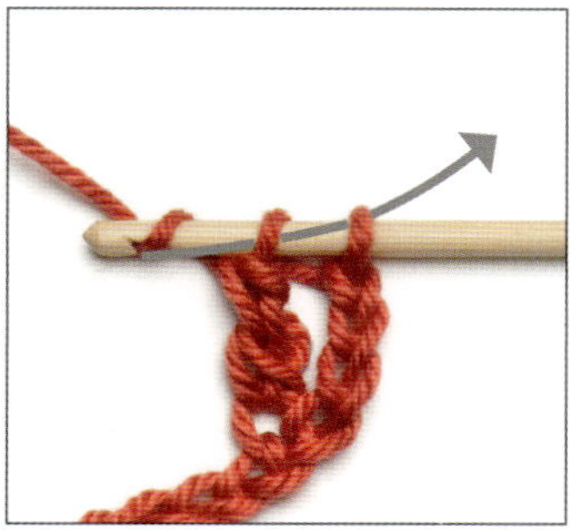

4. Two loops are left. Catch the yarn around the hook and draw it through both loops.

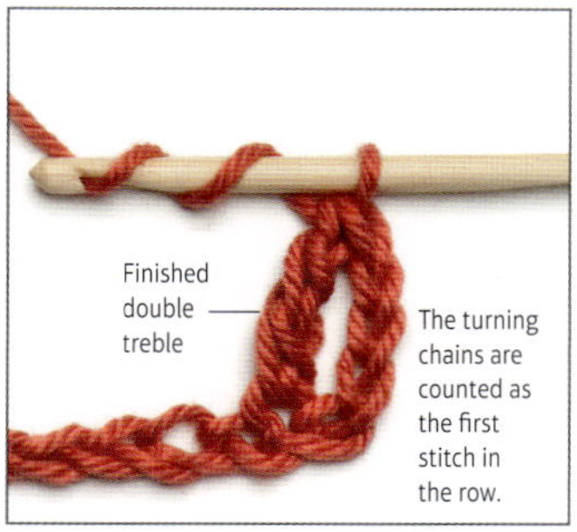

5. The first double treble is complete. Start the following rows with four chain stitches.

Triple treble

Every treble variation with a higher number is worked according to the same principle as the double treble: all that changes is the number of loops at the beginning and the number of turning chains required.

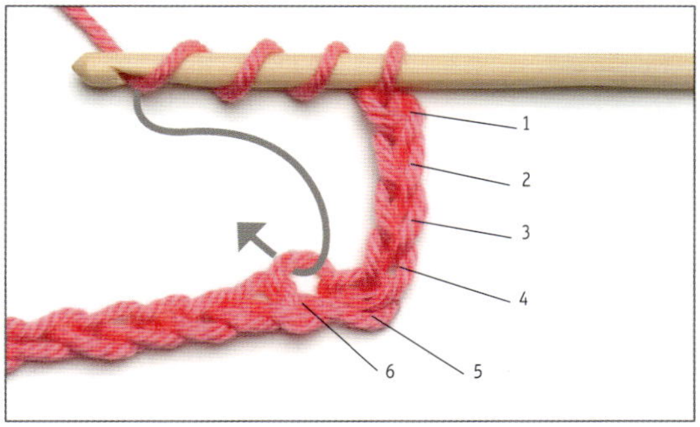

1. Wrap the yarn around the hook three times. Insert the hook into the sixth chain (counting from the hook).

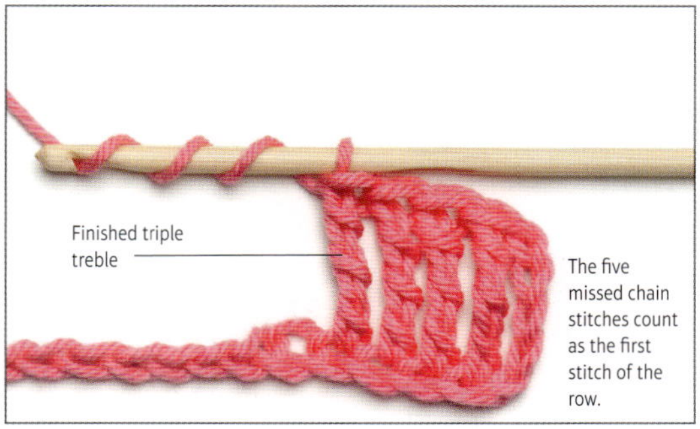

2. Draw the working yarn onto the hook through two loops at a time. Continue until only one loop remains on the hook. Start the following rows with five chains.

Raised treble crochet front

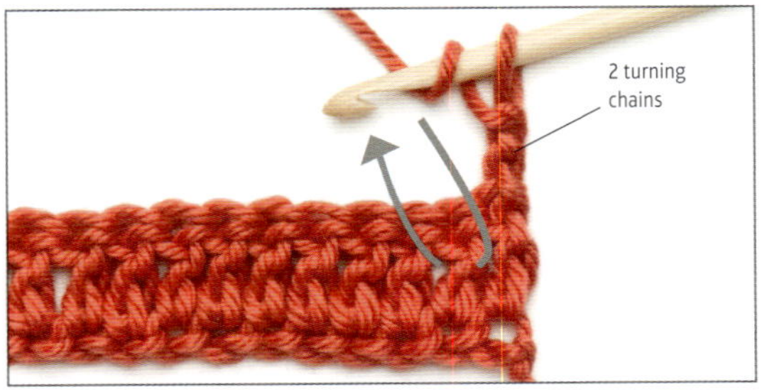

If you make trebles around the post at the front, it creates a rib-like texture.

1. Work the first row as trebles. Start the second row as follows: 2 ch, yarn round hook. Do not insert the hook into the top of the stitch of the previous row as normal, but instead go through the whole treble of the previous row. To do this, insert the hook through from right front to back, and then bring it back again to the left front of the treble (see arrow).

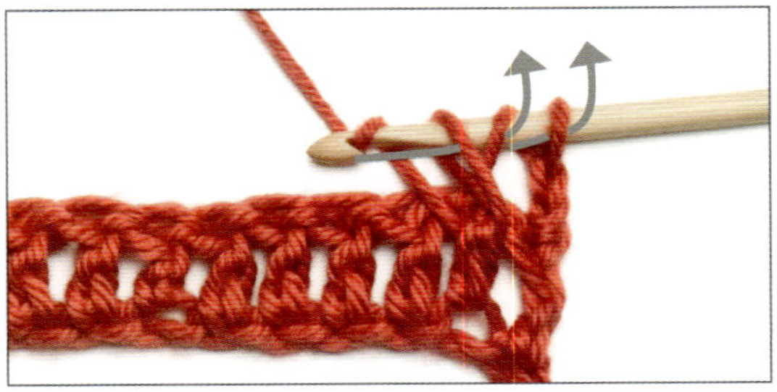

2. Draw a loop through. Then draw the yarn twice through two stitches on the hook at a time (see arrows) to finish the treble as normal (fasten off).

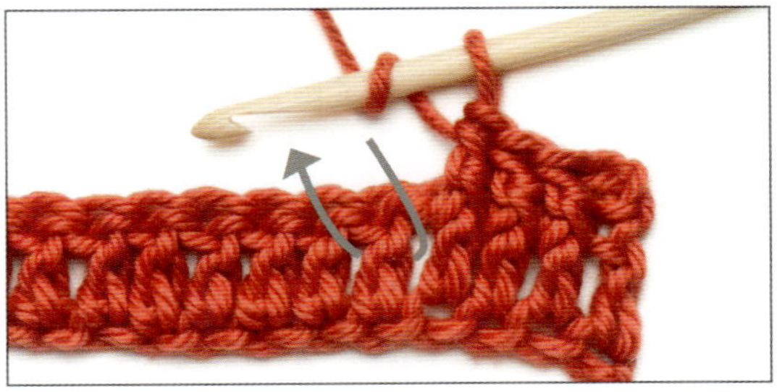

3. Work trebles in the same way around every following treble of the previous row. At the end of the row work a treble in the top turning stitch. Repeat the second row to give a rib-like texture.

Raised treble back

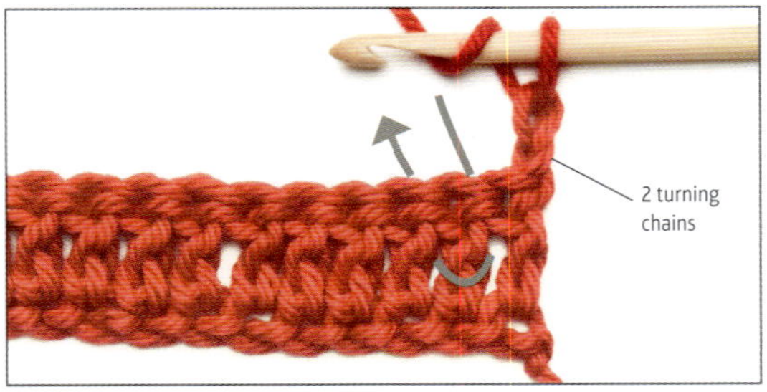

1. Work the first row as trebles. Begin the second row with two chain stitches and the yarn round the hook. Do not insert into the stitch of the previous row as normal, but instead go through the whole treble of the previous row. To do this, insert the hook from back right to the front, then take it through to the back again on the left side of the treble (see arrow).

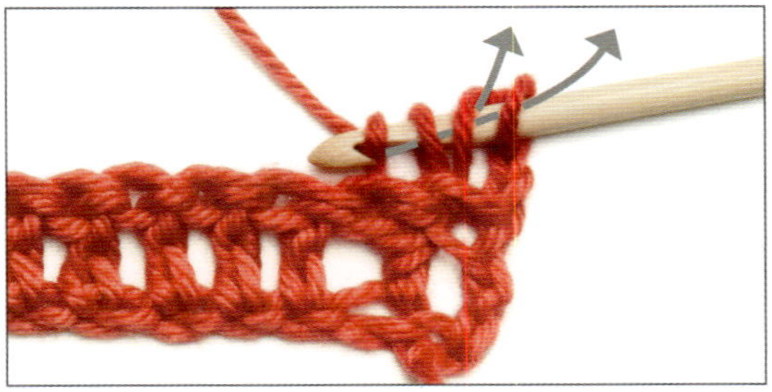

2. Pull a loop through. Then draw the yarn twice through two stitches on the hook at a time (see arrows) to finish the treble.

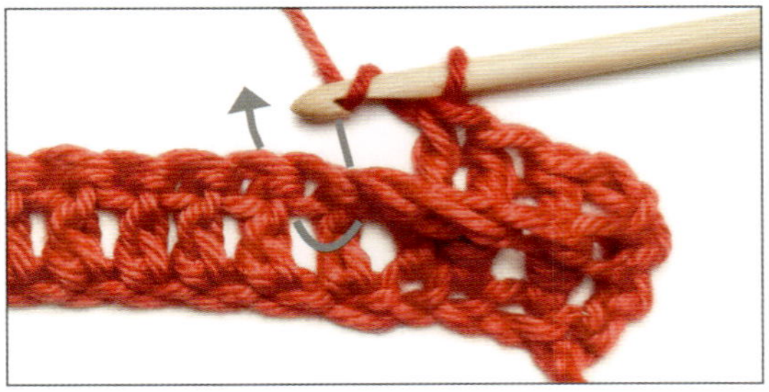

3. Work around every treble of the previous row in the same way. Continue as per step 3 above.

Double crochet decrease

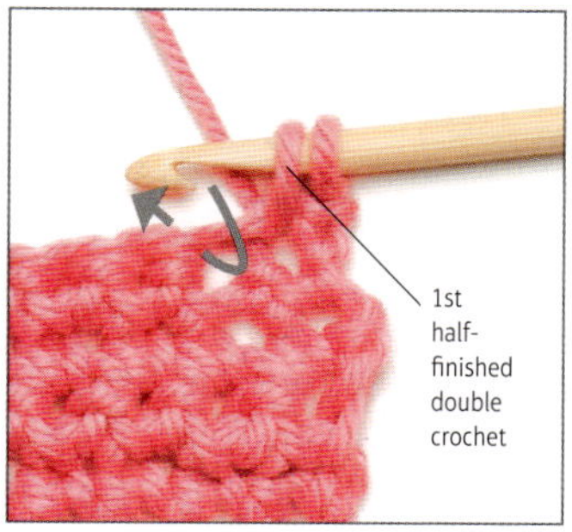

1. To decrease a stitch, make a loop for the stitch as normal, but do not finish off the stitch. You now have two loops on the hook. Insert the hook into the next stitch and make another loop.

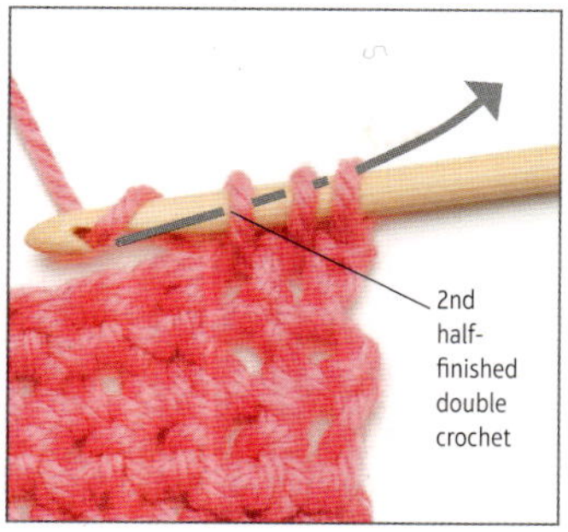

2. There are now three loops on the hook. Catch the working yarn around the hook and draw it through all three loops. This has made one stitch from two double crochets.

Treble decrease

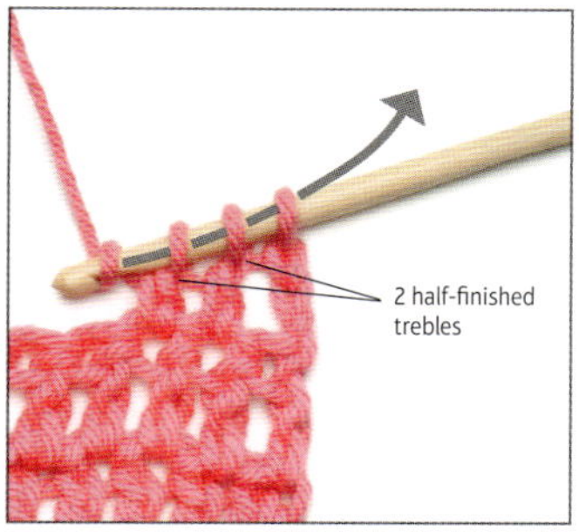

1. Work a half-finished treble, and do the same in the next stitch. Then draw the yarn through all three loops on the hook.

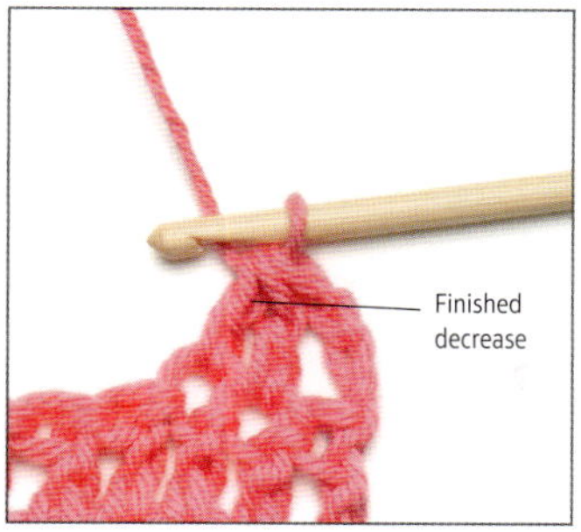

2. Two trebles are now combined into one, that is a stitch has been decreased.

Working rounds into a foundation ring

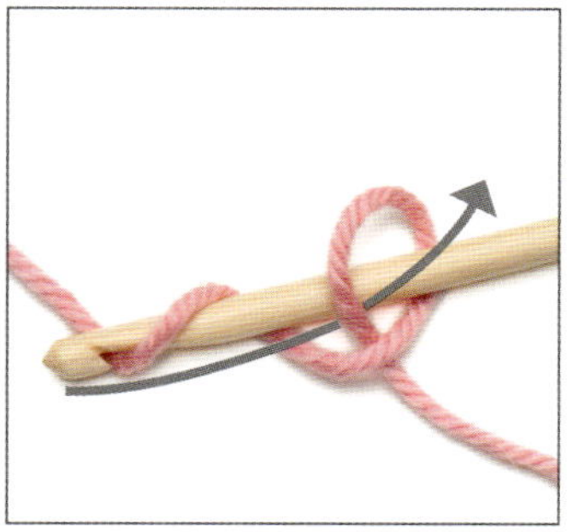

The foundation ring is a quick and simple cast-on method for flat shapes worked in the round. It allows you to adjust the hole in the centre.

1. Make a loop in the yarn and pull the working strand through.

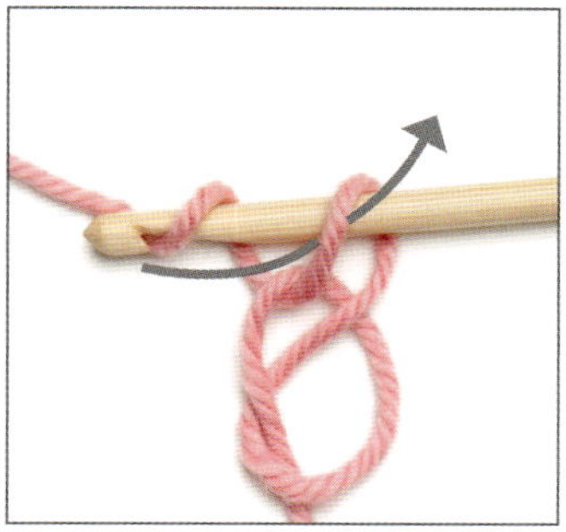

2. Do not pull the loop closed. To begin the first round, work a chain stitch in the loop.

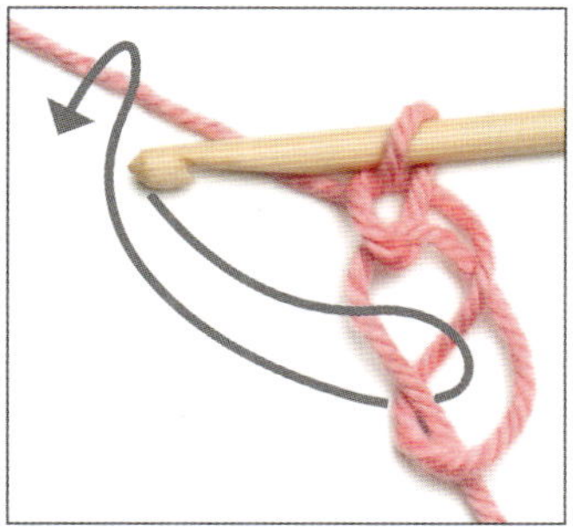

3. Work a double crochet into the loop in the first round, working in the yarn end (see arrow).

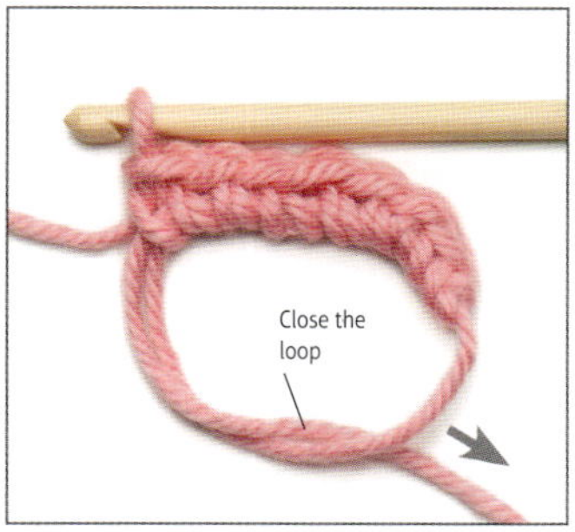

4. When every stitch of the first round is worked, pull the loop together at the yarn end. Then continue to follow the pattern instructions.

Hanna Charlotte Erhorn is an author and industrial designer who specializes in textiles. After graduating from the Hochschule für bildende Künste (University of Fine Arts) in Hamburg she began her career in the exciting world of interior design, working as a stylist for well-known German magazines including *Brigitte*, *Living at Home*, *Schöner Wohnen*, *Vital*, and *essen&trinken*. Her main focus is anything related to DIY, crafts, and home improvements. She lives in Hamburg with her husband, two young sons, and a cat.

Maike Jessen became a freelance photographer in 1997 after training in portrait photography. She has introduced a playful, creative element into her specialist area of work: photographing food and interiors. Her clients include magazines and publishers, as well as PR and advertizing agencies.

Acknowledgements

We are very grateful to Coats and Schachenmayr for their support in producing this book.
Coats GmbH Kenzingen
www.coatsgmbh.de
www.schachenmayr.com

DORLING KINDERSLEY
London, New York, Melbourne, Munich, and Delhi

Dorling Kindersley Verlag
Publishing director Monika Schlitzer
Project editor Bettina Gratzki
Production manager Dorothee Whittaker
Production Anna Ponton

Dorling Kindersely UK
Editor Nikki Sims
Project editor Kathryn Meeker
Senior designers Jane Ewart & Glenda Fisher
Designer Charlotte Johnson
Managing editor Penny Smith
Managing art editor Marianne Markham
Senior Producer, Pre-Production Tony Phipps
Producer Che Creasey
Creative technical support Sonia Charbonnier
Art director Jane Bull
Publisher Mary Ling

Translation project management First Edition Translations Ltd
Translators Ann Drummond & Rae Walter

Photographs pages 86–95: Dorling Kindersley
All other photos and cover photo: Maike Jessen
Text, models, and styling: Hanna Charlotte Erhorn
Drawings on pages 27, 65, and 69: Yo Rühmer
Design, typography, production: Greenstuff Design, Iris & Jochen Grün, Munich
Repro: Medienservice Farbsatz, Neuried

First published by Dorling Kindersley Verlag in 2013
First published in Great Britain in 2014 by
Dorling Kindersley Limited, 80 Strand, London WC2R 0RL

Copyright © 2013, 2014 Dorling Kindersley

A Penguin Random House Company

10 9 8 7 6 5 4 3 2 1
001-193528–March/2014

All rights reserved. No part of this publication may be reproduced, stored in a retrieval system, or transmitted in any form or by any means, electronic, mechanical, photocopying, recording, or otherwise, without the prior written permission of the copyright owner.

A CIP catalogue record for this book is available from the British Library.

This edition produced for The Book People Ltd,
Hall Wood Avenue, Haydock, St Helens, WA11 9UL.

ISBN 978-1-4093-5021-7

Printed and bound in China by Leo Paper Products Ltd.

Discover more at
www.dk.com/crafts